Dream House

Learn more about this book and its author by visiting our web site:

www.overboardministries.com

Cover design by Innovative Graphics
www.igprodesign.com

This title is available for your favorite eReader. Visit our web site to choose the format that's right for you.

All comments or requests for information should be sent to:
overboard@overboardministries.com

DEDICATION

To

Barry D. Bandara
my father, my hero.

Georgene H. Bandara
my mother, my prayer warrior.

Bonny, Betty, Becky, Bobby, Brendie, & Bradley
for all the love, loudness, and laughter my siblings
have provided.

Ashley, Holly, & Kailey
each of you brings so much joy to my heart, and
you have given me one of my most cherished titles... *father*.

And To

Candy Bandara
my wife, the mother of my children, and my best friend.
Thank you for helping me build our *Dream House*
and for encouraging me to write this book!
Without you, our home and my life would be so empty!

CONTENTS

With the church full of those who had great intentions and little follow through, my friend, Barry, has stayed faithful. It is from his Christ-like integrity that I strongly endorse this book. Reader, you will greatly enjoy the practical, engaging, witty, and straight up wisdom from a man who has faithfully lived out what he has written. Bottom line - this book on family issues is abstracted right from the timeless Word of Truth and is delivered from a man that has lived out this truth before other families as well as his own.

Dr. Richard Brown, Assistant Professor
Liberty University, School of Religion
Lynchburg, VA

* * * * *

Here's a book for all of us, including us guys! From those just starting out, to some who are starting over, to others who have lost their way, and especially for those who have never seen what they are trying to build, this will get you back on track to being that good husband and great dad you have always wanted to be. Written in "guy" language (with metaphors and directions we understand), *Dream House* is the manual for the builder in each of us. Follow directions and you will be very happy (and the envy of your friends) with how your project turns out. There is a blueprint for building families and Barry, nearing the end of his own construction efforts, is a master technician.

Dave Carder, MFT, Pastor of Marriage and Counseling Ministries,
First Evangelical Free Church, Fullerton, CA
Author of Unlocking Your Family Patterns and Torn Asunder

* * * * *

Dream House takes on one of the greatest challenges to Christian parents today: bringing up a family that follows the Lord wholeheartedly. Barry Bandara does a stellar job of providing common sense and practical advice that parents can apply, whether their children are one or twenty-one. From time in "The Kitchen" getting nourished to the discipline needed in the "Laundry Room", we are provided with easy-to-remember household illustrations that parents can easily apply. A must read for every parent.

Cliff Carey, Director of Church Relations
Hume Lake Christian Camp
Hume, CA

* * * * *

Most of our Christian lives are not lived in depths of theological contemplation, but in the practical application of the truths we hold dear. In his book, Barry looks at our Christianity where the rubber meets the road...in our lives as husband, wives, fathers and mothers. Perhaps our most simple, but significant expression of who we are in Christ is found in the roles we play in our family. This tour through the "dream house" leaves the reader with lots of opportunity for reflection on how their own houses measure up to God's ideal, and then offers practical advice for our own home improvement.

Kevin Hearne, Pastor of Adult Ministries
Community Bible Church
Central Point, OR

* * * * *

Barry Bandara's Dream House: Blueprints to a Healthy and Happy Home is a much-needed book. It is engaging, fast-paced, and entertaining from beginning to end, which makes it fun to read; but it is also packed with vital information so badly needed by today's families who are struggling to survive in this post modern culture. The author offers up helpful and timeless truths from God's Word, which are often considered unpalatable by many, but the way he cleverly presents them as we stroll through his Dream House (like Mary Poppin's spoon-full of sugar) really helps the medicine go down.

Ted Duncan, Senior Pastor
Calvary Bible Church, Bakersfield, CA
Author of A Snowball's Chance and God's Revenge

* * * * *

Barry is passionate, about his marriage, his family and most importantly, about God. Dream House does a masterful job of laying out God's plan for a happy home, which is something we strive for everyday. Being a husband and father myself I was drawn to the resources, stories and practical applications of how Barry lives this out on a daily basis. If you are looking for a wonderful book for your future family, the Dream House has everything you need.

Kevin Scruggs, communicator/Executive Pastor
Bayside Church, South Sacramento, CA
Contributing author of Nelson's Church Leader's Manual

* * * * *

Barry Bandara is a man who "walks the talk." Not only has he successfully modeled his own advice at home, he has successfully mentored it in ministry. The "blueprints" in Dream House are a "must read" for anyone who wants to move beyond a virtual tour to a reality construction of the kind of house that God can build. All together now: "Move that bus!"

Dr. Curt DeGraaff, Senior Pastor,
Bethesda Baptist Church, Brownsburg, IN

ACKNOWLEDGMENTS

Lindsay Manchester – my ministry assistant and friend who encouraged me throughout this whole book writing process. Thank you for your encouragement and support!

Brenda Noland – my editor who made this book happen. Thank you for your detailed work, sense of humor, and for pushing me for clarity when needed. You have become a friend.

To all my **former students** in ministry - some of you made it into this book, although I changed some of your names to protect your guilt...I mean innocence.

To **Linn Winters** at Cornerstone Church - although we have never met, your *Family Matters* series sparked the room-to-room concept for this book.

To the encouraging church family and staff at **GracePoint Church** - it is an honor to teach God's Word and serve alongside of you. Thank you for helping us *"build a vibrant church that attracts the unchurched"* in Kitsap County.

Foreword

From three very blessed daughters...

Ever since our dad had the inspiration to write a book about building strong, godly families, we would constantly see him at his desk, during his day off, typing passionately away on his computer. He has poured his heart and soul into each and every chapter, with the hope of helping other families.

We are so blessed to say that God has provided us a godly father who gives his absolute best in all areas of his life. He attends every single one of our basketball games, is a supportive audience member at our plays and productions, and comes home from a stressful day at work still willing to engage in our lives. Our dad's sense of humor has helped him live in a female world filled with makeup, emotions, chick flicks and ballet tutus. In the midst of it all, he still manages to preach three messages every weekend! We can simply say: Our dad rocks!

Although our family is far from perfect, our dad has done his very best to discipline, love and encourage us even during the difficult times – especially during our teenage years. And he couldn't have done it without God's strength and direction, and of course without the help of our wonderful godly mom! Our parents always taught us the value of character while growing up. When we three girls were little, we would hear, "Girls, play nicely and share your Barbies," and even now as teenagers we still hear, "Girls, ask your sister first before you take her outfit from her closet." Our dad has definitely modeled a godly example of how a man should treat his family. He constantly shows our mom affection and love, and all three of us girls can proudly say that we want to marry a man like our dad someday!

We hope that you will be able to hear our dad's heart and passion for marriages and families. We want you to be able to hear his voice and character throughout this book just like we have heard growing up. We also want you to be able to walk away with a better understanding of how to construct a "Dream House" with God's direction.

We love you, Dad!
~Ashley, Holly, and Kailey Bandara

Introduction

Have you ever visited the Land of "What If?"

What if we had more money? *What if* we lived in a bigger house? *What if* we could live without the constant grind of financial pressure? *What if?* If you're anything like me, I'm sure you know this land well, and like me, you've taken many walks down its street of magical mirages.

In 2001, my family and I were living in affluent Orange County on a single income. As you can imagine, this resulted in a very tight budget with little to no margin for extras – forget about tickets to Disneyland, frequent meals out, or plenty of new clothes for growing girls. And as far as emergency savings, we just had to hope and pray that nobody did anything that required stitches or crutches! The home we were renting was clean and adequate to meet our needs, but I was tempted to dream about a nicer, larger home for my family – our very own Dream House. On a youth pastor's salary, dreaming was all I could afford!

Sometimes I'd surprise my three young daughters on the way home from church by taking them on a model home tour in one of the newly built housing developments in the Fullerton, Yorba Linda, and Brea area where we lived. When we pulled into a new development with houses worth close to a million dollars, our oil-leaking, sputtering, non-air-conditioned 1986 Honda was a dead giveaway that we were not potential buyers. Not even close. But to tell the truth, we didn't care! We were there to dream.

We enjoyed pretending that the new home we were touring was actually *our* home! In our dream world, we'd drive past our immaculately landscaped front yard into a three-car garage (heated, of course). When we made our entrance into our fully furnished 3500-square-foot mansion, we'd be greeted with wall-to-wall hardwood floors, crown molding, multiple fireplaces, spiraling staircases, and a balcony for quiet reading. Our kitchen would have granite countertops, stainless steel appliances, a breakfast nook, and an open view to the rest of the living area. The entertainment room would boast a surround-sound system on steroids, with a television big enough to fulfill any man's sports viewing fantasies.

My girls loved to hurry upstairs to claim "their" bedrooms. They no longer had to share a single crowded bedroom, because each of the three girls had already mentally moved into a full-size plush room of her own, with its own bathroom to match. I also enjoyed visiting the Land of What If, since "my" master bedroom flaunted vaulted ceilings, a private balcony, and its own fireplace. Instead of taking turns with one sink as we brushed our teeth and got ready for the day, Candy and I would have his-and-hers vanity areas inside a master bathroom to die for!

After taking our time savoring every room of "our house," we eventually walked out of our dream world, climbed back into reality, put on our seat belts, and headed home. We all knew the truth – there was no way we could ever afford to live in such an amazing house. But we could dream, couldn't we?

A Real Dream

The recession of 2008 and beyond caused a great deal of pain and suffering throughout American culture. The real estate market saw record numbers of home foreclosures, short sales, and bankruptcies as a result of a severe drop in home values. Many people lost faith in Wall Street as they watched much of their retirement portfolio evaporate when the stock market crashed. In the midst of this, one positive change rose out of the ashes of this economic turmoil. There was a renewed focus on what is of real importance and of real value in life: the family.

The book you are holding has nothing to do with the physical structures in which families live. After all, every housing structure will eventually deteriorate and have to be torn down. But our families and our family heritage can have real and lasting value, if they are built properly on a solid foundation.

Many people today are the product of a dysfunctional home. Their families were built on a foundation of abuse, anger, arguments, divorce, selfishness, neglect, and disrespect. This is what family means to them. This is their "normal." But when someone from a dysfunctional home comes in close contact with a family demonstrating love, honor, respect, joy, and genuine kindness, they can't help but be taken aback by the visible contrast with their own home.

Just as I thought the new houses we toured in Orange County were only a dream, there are many who believe their deep-down desire for a healthy and happy home is just that – a dream.

Let me encourage you – there is hope! The institution of the home was not established by a blue-ribbon panel of politicians or philosophers. Can you imagine how different the family would look if that was the case? Can you envision the layers of pointless regulation and needless bureaucracy? The family would be in far worse condition than it already is!

The institution of the home was established by God. He is the architectural designer of the family, and His blueprints remain reliable for every new generation. Even when life throws unexpected challenges that cause harm to our families, we have a dependable set of plans that will help our homes get back on the road to health.

When people see my family and the atmosphere of love and health in our home, it isn't because we're so smart and have it all figured out. Believe me, I don't have it all figured out, and I'm the first to admit I might not be the sharpest tool in the toolbox.

In fact, some days I can barely *spell* IQ! No, the reason for the health and happiness in our home all comes back to our choice to build our Dream House following God's blueprints.

My Story

I loved my grandpa, Alfred. I have fond boyhood memories of being allowed to steer his VW Bug as he was driving around his neighborhood. He'd also chase our family car down the street whenever we'd leave his house after a visit. I'd laugh and wave goodbye, twisting around in my seat to see him out the back window as he ran after us with his goofy grin. However, although he could comfortably relate to us grandkids, he had a difficult time connecting with his own children. My father told me that Grandpa was never the same after he returned from World War II. He was content to quietly go to work as a sign painter, come home, and read the paper, disengaging from life and his family.

I also loved my grandmother, Enid. She showered all of us grandkids with love and attention in all kinds of ways – kisses, delicious meals, and even showing up at my basketball games from time to time. But let me tell you - she was a piece of work! She was a dominant woman who expressed her opinion on any and every topic, whether you asked for it or not. You did not cross her. You did not debate her, and if you were brave enough to try, you did not win. She was always right, about everything. Or so she thought, and so did you, if you knew what was good for you.

My father grew up with an overwhelming sense of rejection. Grandma Enid's parents made their opinion clear to her that she should have stopped having children after my Uncle Eddie, my dad's older brother, was born. To drive their point home, when Christmas came my dad's grandparents brought presents, but only for Eddie. When birthdays came there were more gifts – but just for Eddie, not for my father. Year after year this continued. After growing up with a disengaged father, an overbearing mother, and grandparents who ignored and rejected him, my dad struggled daily with his sense of self-worth.

In ninth grade, baseball changed his life. In fact, he once told me that baseball "rescued him." The sport helped him escape from his life at home and from the demons of rejection. He'd play every chance he got, and he quickly became very good. He was fast, he could get on base, and he'd run down every fly ball hit anywhere in his vicinity. Baseball, bringing with it a much-needed sense of accomplishment and self-worth, was oxygen to his soul.

But off the baseball field he continued to struggle with self-confidence. While he was close to his older brother and younger sister, my father would never in his life hear the words "I love you" from his father. Over time, his mother's strong opinions and dominance wore him down. He once told me that he would only invite a few of his closest friends over, because he was embarrassed to bring any more friends to his house. Why? His home was not healthy.

When he was in his early twenties, my father (Barry) met my mother (Georgene) and they eventually married. They didn't waste much time in starting their family. Between their busy life with young children and the unhealthy pattern of marriage my dad had seen, my parents didn't have a deep and connected relationship with each other. But everything changed the day Jesus Christ became their Savior. New blueprints were unrolled and construction began on their Dream House.

Because of this, my home life was very different from my dad's. My parents raised seven children – Bonny, Barry, Betty, Becky, Bobby, Brendie, and Bradley. Our home was large, loud, and overflowing with love. It was a place filled with security, confidence, and health. It wasn't just us kids, either - we had friends over all the time! Rick, one of my friends in junior high, surprised me one day with a comment about my home. He said, "I'm jealous of you. I wished I lived in a home like yours." It stunned me because Rick had so many things I envied: a rich family, a pool in his backyard, new clothes and nice cars. It was the first time I realized that I too had something incredibly valuable that I'd taken for granted all that time: my home!

With such a large family, we had our problems, too. All families do. Look deeper into the back story of my home when I was growing up, and you'll find a narrative touched by tears, sadness, and tragedy just like that of most families today. But none of us seven Bandara kids would trade our home for the world!

Now I have a family of my own. My wife, Candy, and I have three girls – Ashley, Holly, and Kailey. We call Ashley our "drama queen" because of her flair for the dramatic and her love for the arts and theater. Holly and Kailey are our sports chicks, and we've spent many hours cheering them on at their basketball, volleyball, and softball games. We have been blessed to build upon the foundation laid by our parents, and we've tried to provide a healthy and happy home for our girls – one that will carry into the next generation and beyond.

Every year, the various members of the Bandara bunch travel from the four western states of Washington, Oregon, California and Arizona to Medford, Oregon to get together for Thanksgiving. All 28 of us invade my sister's home for three days of food, laughter, prayer, competition, and retelling stories from the past. Although we usually come away exhausted, there is a lingering sense of amazement and appreciation at how blessed we are to all have healthy and happy homes. In today's culture, this kind of home is rare. To some, it is a Dream House.

War on the Family
Ever since the first home came on the market when Adam and Eve set up house together, Satan has waged war against the family. In Genesis 3 we witness blame and finger-pointing between the first husband and wife. In Genesis 4 the first two brothers' ongoing conflicts eventually ended in bloodshed. The attack on the home continues to this day, seen in homes marked

by yelling, fighting, running away, divorce, lying, broken promises, unforgiving attitudes, strife, conflict, physical violence, shouting, swearing, and abuse. We hear these kinds of comments: "Don't tell me what to do!" "I'm not listening to you!" "I hate you!" "Get out of my house!" "Shut up!", and on and on. And that's just describing many *Christian* homes!

The home is the bedrock of every civilization and culture. The stronger the home, the stronger the society will be. If our homes are weak, dysfunctional, and unstable, our culture will reflect this as well.

It doesn't take more than a quick glance at our society to see that our homes and our culture are in shambles. Multiple generations have grown up without ever having firsthand experience of a healthy home. Millions of men have no idea of what a healthy husband and father look like. The same is true for countless women when it comes to being a healthy wife and mother.

Something has to change! If not, the baggage of one bad home will be carried out the front door and unloaded onto the living room floor of the next new marriage, and the cycle will start over again with the next generation. This cycle must stop. Our homes need help. We need a new blueprint for our homes, and we need it now.

New Construction

Whenever you see a healthy and happy family, it's not because of where they live or what they own. When you see a healthy and happy home, it is a result of hard, consistent, diligent work. It is the result of a long series of right choices that develop into right habits.

As a pastor for over 25 years, I've seen lots of different kinds of homes. I've been in apartments in the inner city projects on streets that were scary to drive through at night. I've also visited multimillion-dollar waterfront homes with beautiful interiors and perfectly maintained grounds, and I've been in many houses between those two extremes. Some of these homes have been healthy. Many were not. This book is an attempt to provide a blueprint for you to build a healthy and happy home for your own family, and for the generations to come.

I will not deal in theory. We will stay in the realm of truth, providing practical everyday examples. I am not calling us to return to the wishful thinking of the *Leave it to Beaver* model for our homes. However, I am calling us to go back to God's blueprints – a return to time-tested truths and principles from God's Word that work every time they are followed!

From the kitchen to the garage, we will walk through key principles that will help make your home healthy and happy. As we walk through the corridors of this house you may be encouraged to realize, "We are on the right path!" Others may receive confirmation that "We have some remodeling to do!" Regardless, every healthy and happy home requires hard work and comes with a significant price tag that is paid in time, energy, and sacrifice. Take heart – it is worth the effort!

Before You Read

You need to know that my home is not perfect. It's a house with parents who are sinful and selfish, and who inevitably passed along these bad qualities to their three children. Our Dream House has had its share of arguments, hurt feelings, disobedience, tears, and plenty of "will you forgive me?" moments. As you read, please remember that we are still building our house. We have the hardhats and sawdust to prove it.

For those of you who are single parents, I understand the uphill challenge you face as a parent. In some ways you are trying to parent with one hand tied behind your back as you don't have another parent providing additional support, encouragement, and perspective. In divorce situations where there are court ordered parenting plans, visitation rights, or stepparents involved, this can really complicate what you are trying to accomplish as a parent. I have often seen children using emotional power over a parent when they keep a copy of their "I want to live with my dad" or "You are *not* my mom!" card in their back pocket at all times. This can put a great deal of pressure on a parent to capitulate to the desires of the child out of fear of losing them.

I have also experienced many situations where one parent, out of love, puts down much-needed boundaries and guardrails for their children, only to be undermined by the irresponsible "fun" parent who appears to be buying their children's loyalty with few to no rules when the kids come to their house. Let me encourage you to continue to do the best you can with the resources and energy you have. Ask God to bring along healthy role models to come alongside your children. As hard as it is at times, resist the urge to criticize the other parent in front of your kids. Speak the truth, but do so with discernment and respect. Your children will eventually respect you all the more because you took the honorable path.

Regardless of your family situation, this book is not a black and white book, nor does it contain all shades of grey. No book can. If I don't cover your exact family or parenting situation, look for the truthful principles within each chapter.

Remember that the principles in each chapter are just that – principles. Each family must redesign their house according to their unique situation. However, truthful principles are transferable. Whether your family is comprised of two parents or single parents, and whether it has biological, step, and/or adopted children, these truths and principles are adaptable to your home. Overlap these blueprints onto your current home environment, and build accordingly.

So put on your hard hat, adjust your tool belt, pour yourself a cup of coffee, and roll up your sleeves. Let's get to work on your home!

Small Group Questions:

1. What's the "What If" Land that you find yourself visiting?

2. Describe your family heritage. What is the back story of your home life when you were growing up?

3. What is your definition of "normal" family life?

4. What areas of your home and family do you need help with?

"Sometimes you struggle so hard to feed your family one way, you forget to feed them the other way, with spiritual nourishment."
James Brown

Chapter One
The Kitchen: Nourishment

My wife and girls love to watch the home shows that have recently flooded the cable airwaves. There are shows that help first-time buyers purchase their first home, shows that remodel on the cheap, and shows that flip houses. The ones that get me are those where neighbors compete against each other to see who can get the best return on their investment after spending $90,000 to remodel their bathroom! Are you kidding me? Since I love seeing what people can do with their homes using their own money, I can vicariously experience their home shopping and remodeling without spending a dime.

Regardless of the budget or the remodeling style, though, one principle comes up time and again in these home shows – the kitchen makes or breaks the home. Why? It is the heart of the home, the place where family life happens. Remove the kitchen and all you have is a glorified motel room. It doesn't matter how cool I think the man cave is – if my wife doesn't like the kitchen, the sale won't go down!

The kitchen is often conveniently located in the center of the home because it is at the crossroads of everyone's daily routine. Family members are coming and going, talking, cooking, and eating together. This also is why the kitchen is often the most cluttered room in the home. It never gets a break!

Along with being Grand Central Station in most homes, the kitchen is also the primary source for nourishment in every healthy home. Physically speaking, it's where the food is stored, prepared, and served. When we can't sleep at night, where do we go? We wander out to the kitchen to find something to eat. When the kids come home from a long day at school, what do they do? They drop their backpacks by the door with a floor-shaking thud and immediately head to the kitchen. They open the refrigerator and cabinet doors, ready to inhale anything they can find. (Is it just me, or do your kids stand there with the fridge door open for an eternity?) The kitchen grows gradually colder as they peer into a refrigerator packed from top to bottom with groceries and whine, "How come there's nothing to eat?"

Although I never took a home economics class, I'm at least aware of the five basic food groups:

1. Bread and cereals that provide us with carbohydrates and fiber
2. Fruits and vegetables that give us vitamins and minerals
3. Milk and dairy that supply our bodies with calcium
4. Meat, fish and beans that give us protein
5. Fat and sugar that add flavor to our diet

Although every home includes a kitchen, many homes are not providing the proper nourishment for their family. Cupboards are filled with sugar, fats, salt, and everybody's favorite box of sugary toasted goodness – Pop-Tarts! Between the greasy bags of chips at home and the routine meals of drive-through fast food, it's no wonder our country is facing an obesity crisis.

Beyond food groups, calories and fat intake, what builds a healthy, well-nourished home? Well, let's take a closer look at the word *nourishment*, which of course comes from the word *nourish*. (Have I lost anyone yet?) This word has a two-fold definition: "to promote growth; to sustain with nutrients." A healthy home is one that consistently provides the necessary ingredients to promote physical, emotional, relational, and spiritual growth to all who live under its roof. With a home like this, a family will be sustained for many years to come.

Unpacking this word further, the English word *nourish* comes from the Latin *nutrire*, which means literally "to feed." Over time, however, as the word passed through the Middle English *norisshe* into the form we use today, it picked up the additional meanings of sustaining life in other ways than the physical – strengthening, building up, and cultivating the mind and soul as well as the body. This expanded definition helps us to move beyond food and in the direction of what makes a house into a healthy home with the proper nourishment.

Four Types of Nourishment
A Healthy Marriage

It is often said, "The best gift you can ever give your children is to love your spouse." Parents can give their kids toys, iPods, sports equipment, and the latest and coolest gadget, only to have it all eventually break or get lost in the mysterious black hole that exists inside of every house. Garages are cluttered with castaway junk that was all, at one time, someone's prized possession.

Many parents attempt to make wise financial investments, intending to someday pass on the fruits of these investments to their children. There is nothing wrong with this strategy. But the best and wisest investment, the one that is guaranteed to make a lasting impression on your children, is to give them the gift of a healthy marriage. It will result in huge benefits for your children, and likely for generations to come.

When children see their parents displaying a healthy marriage, it provides an emotional foundation that will sustain them for the rest of their lives. Although they won't realize it at the time, they are being nourished (trained) for their own future marriage. Boys will overtly and subtly be shown how a man loves a woman, and their watchful minds will be filing away qualities they desire in a future wife. Girls will have their relational checklist filled out with attractive qualities for their future husband. Most likely, they will later mimic their mother's behavior when they become a wife one day. This is sustaining nourishment in the highest degree!

Proverbs 31 is an excellent example of sustaining nourishment in the home. This Scripture is traditionally taught as a women's-only kind of a chapter. But a woman didn't write this chapter – a man did! So, heads up, guys. Even though you may have heard this Proverb directed toward your mom, your sister, or your wife, the author is talking to men too!

The author's name was King Lemuel, and this chapter is the only place he is mentioned in the Bible. Although no one knows for sure, some believe it was a pen name for King Solomon, or possibly King Hezekiah. Regardless of his actual identity, his words are powerful, noble, and worthy of emulating in any marriage. In verse 10, King Lemuel begins with beautiful words of affirmation from a husband to his wife. He says:

> *"A wife of noble character who can find? She is worth far more than rubies. Her husband has full confidence in her and lacks nothing of value. She brings him good, not harm, all the days of her life. Her children arise and call her blessed; her husband also, and he praises her." (Proverbs 31:10-12, 28)*

This husband doesn't hesitate to brag about his wife. He declares that she is precious and valuable to him, and he affirms his utmost confidence and trust in her. He cannot help but praise his wife for who she is and for the tremendous role she plays in his life. In return, this greatly cherished woman responds to her husband with encouragement, respect, and faithfulness.

I admit it – I love embarrassing my wife. I love seeing her get that uncomfortable squirm when I unashamedly brag on her in front of my kids. Out of the blue I'll say, "Your mom is incredible! I am so glad your mom said 'yes' when I asked her to marry me!" And when I add, "And did I ever tell you that your mom is *hot*?", it always brings the tilted head and her predictable, laughing response – "Barry, stop!" – along with a smile that says, "But thank you!"

When I celebrate my wife for who she is and for all that she does inside and outside our home, these compliments are not just for my wife to hear. They are also directed toward the ears of my daughters. I want my girls to know how much their mom does for our family and how much she is appreciated, adored, and loved by their father.

In return, I appreciate how Candy respects me in front of my daughters. She blesses me with words of encouragement and smiles of affirmation, and by going out of her way to make me want to come home after a long day at church. Although my wife doesn't necessarily enjoy sharing me with all the demands that go along with my work as a pastor, she fully believes in what God has called me to do. She does whatever it takes to model her love and support for me. Therefore, taking Mom's cue, my girls believe that what God has called me to do – being a pastor – is a great thing!

A healthy marriage also provides nourishment to our children by showing appropriate public affection. I believe it is important for a mom and a dad to demonstrate their love in front of their children. Thus, hugging and kissing is commonplace in our home. Most days I come home from work and head straight to Candy for a kiss. When our girls were young, they'd moan in embarrassment, "Mom! Dad! Don't do that!" Of course that would only encourage me to do it all the more, with added flair! Now that they are older, our girls think nothing of Candy and I kissing, hugging, holding hands, and snuggling during a movie. We want the DNA of our continued romance to be passed on to their future marriages.

My father served as a youth pastor for a while in the early 1970's. As I headed into my own ministry as a youth pastor in the late 1980's, I still remember the first piece of ministry advice he gave me. As we sat together in my office, he said simply, "Create memories for your students." Now, after 20 years in youth ministry, there are plenty of sermons, trips, camps, skits, and activities for my former students to remember. But what I am finding through their emails and Facebook posts is that one significant memory stands out to them – *our marriage.*

It wasn't that our marriage was perfect. It wasn't then, and it isn't today! My students had front-row seats when Candy and I got on each other's nerves. I recall an incident in the early stages of one long, sleep-deprived trip where Candy was giving instructions to a youth group ministry team, and my fatigued brain thought it would be a good idea to chip in with, "Can you repeat what you said? It wasn't clear." She replied, "If you were paying attention, you'd have gotten it the first time." I shot back, "Well, obviously you didn't communicate clearly or I wouldn't have - " and stopped short as I finally registered what the students were doing during this tender, loving exchange. All 40 of them were listening avidly, their heads snapping back and forth between us like spectators at a tennis match. I couldn't help but laugh, and the students' answering laughter broke the tension of what was probably *not* one of our finest moments. I'm sure this wasn't the only incident when we weren't at our best, but what they remember is a steady diet of love, respect, affection, and laughter in our relationship.

Our children need the unique emotional and relational nourishment that a healthy marriage can provide. They not only need it, they *deserve* it. We must equip them with a marital blueprint for their emotional and relational growth, and for sustaining nourishment in their lives. The "kitchen" in our homes must have cupboards that are overflowing with marital nutrients such as love, respect, affection, date nights, kindness, encouragement, laughter, tenderness, and honor.

The three remaining types of nourishment in our homes are important and essential. But if the marriage in the home is damaged or unhealthy, the other three ingredients lose their vitality, power, and effectiveness. While it's not impossible, it is certainly difficult for a couple with an unhealthy marriage to provide the proper nourishment for a healthy home!

Fortunately, there are many great resources available for any marriage that needs help. I would highly recommend attending a *Family Life: Weekend to Remember* event. This weekend retreat has strengthened thousands of marriages and helped rescue others on the verge of failing. Going to this retreat could be a helpful reminder of why you fell in love with your spouse in the first place. Taking the time to learn valuable marriage-building tools from these experienced teachers would be a significant investment that could reap lasting benefits for your entire family.

Second, read the book *Love and Respect* by Dr. Emerson Eggerichs. I believe it is one of the best marriage books out there, particularly for the way it uses Ephesians 5 to lay out God's original blueprint for the role of a husband and a wife.

One last suggestion: Watch Mark Gungor's video series, *Laugh Your Way to a Better Marriage*. You will indeed laugh, but you will also soak in a variety of practical principles to help your marriage become or remain healthy.

Make a commitment to do whatever it takes to move your marriage from unhealthy to healthy, or from healthy to even healthier. Your kids may cover their eyes and make comments about Public Displays of Affection, but if you put the effort into making and keeping your marriage healthy, they will one day thank you.

Years from now, how will your children describe your marriage? What will they say about what you modeled for them? How will they describe the interaction between their mother and father? Believe me, they'll remember. They will talk about it. What will they say?

I think back on my parents' marriage. They had some good days, some hard days, and some very rocky days. I didn't realize in my preteen years that my parents were going through some major marital battles. But I do remember, as a teenager, how my parents acted once they returned from a trip to Colorado. They were holding hands more often. They were kissing in the kitchen more often. I noticed a change in them immediately, and I found out later that they had made some significant investments that strengthened their marriage while they were on that getaway.

My memories of my grandparents' home are completely different. Alfred and Enid were like cats and dogs, with my domineering grandmother constantly lecturing my grandfather. In return, it appeared that my grandfather's sole aim in life was to irritate that woman. He would wait until the perfect time to say or do something that would cause her to explode, only to beat a hasty retreat behind his newspaper while she blew. As a child, I thought it was hilarious. From my current perspective as an adult, it's not so funny. What a sad way to live life together! Please don't leave this kind of legacy for your children. Let them remember a strong and healthy marriage. Leave them a template they will want to follow.

Let me encourage you if you are a single parent. I have seen scores of single parents do an outstanding job of overcoming the damage left behind by a dysfunctional marriage, or a failed relationship where no marriage ever occurred. These parents were warriors who overcame many obstacles for the health of their children.

One single mother who stands out to me is a woman named Marsha, a faithful member of our church in Vancouver, Washington. She leaned heavily on a strong church and youth group that provided many healthy role models for her son,

Kiyle. I always appreciated Marsha's positive and determined spirit. I never heard her badmouth her former husband.

Although Marsha didn't have a healthy marriage, she provided the next three ingredients in her home for the nourishment of her children. Kiyle ended up marrying a godly young lady from a solid, healthy home, and they now have a great marriage and four beautiful kids. They are well on their way in providing a healthy and happy home that Kiyle did not experience while growing up.

Character Is King

The second nutritious ingredient in the kitchen of a Dream House involves character development. Character is the life skill of doing what is right, all the time, whether anyone is watching or not. Character is not built into our DNA. It must be modeled for us. It must be learned. Parents are teaching and modeling good (or bad) character all the time, whether they're aware of it or not!

The sustaining nutrients of good character will stay with your child for a lifetime. Character is exhibited in many different ways: being truthful and hard-working, having integrity, being reliable and self-motivated, following through with one's responsibilities or promises, having self-control, showing compassion for others, doing your best, and many other instances where inner strength is seen in outward behavior.

Parents often place high value on tangible things like good grades, a clean room, making the team, trophies, awards, getting the part, and on and on. These are all fine, but they are nowhere close to being as valuable as character! Character trumps them all. Character is king. Character is more important than straight A's! It matters more than awards won on the athletic field that will one day sit forgotten on a shelf, gathering dust. Character, however, will continue far into our children's future. It will sustain them throughout their lives in all of their future jobs, relationships, and the many challenges life throws at them.

In the first nine verses of Proverbs 31, King Lemuel remembers words and phrases his mother lovingly repeated while he was growing up, words that still echoed in his ear. Lemuel writes:

> "O my son, O son of my womb, O son of my vows, do not spend your strength on women, your vigor on those who ruin kings. It is not for kings, O Lemuel – not for kings to drink wine, not for rulers to crave beer, lest they drink and forget what the law decrees, and deprive all the oppressed of their rights. Give beer to those who are perishing, wine to those who are in anguish; let them drink and forget their poverty and remember their misery no more. Speak up for those who cannot speak for themselves, for the rights of all who are destitute. Speak up and judge fairly; defend the rights of the poor and needy." (Proverbs 31:2-9)

It's in the fine print of the maternal contract to teach, instruct, remind, lecture, and give words of warning. Mothers can't help themselves: Sit up straight, slouching is bad for your posture! Don't sit so close to the TV, it's bad for your eyes! Eat your vegetables, they're good for you! Drive safely. Buckle your seat belt. Slow down, you're driving too fast!

Mothers continue to be mothers even when their children are grown and have families of their own. Moms still say, "Put a sweater on, it's cold outside. You don't want to catch a cold!" To which the son replies, "Yes, Mom! I'm fifty-seven years old! I know!"

King Lemuel's mother gave him wise counsel that he never forgot. She emphasized good character traits with advice such as:

- Don't be a womanizer (verse 3).
- Stay level-headed and sober (verse 4-5).

- Always be looking for ways to help others (verse 8).
- Be a leader (verse 9).
- Help those who are helpless (verse 9).

All of these instructions are character-based. She knew he would one day be the king, so she drove home these lessons in character long before that royal day arrived.

As parents, we must recognize that one day our children will leave our home and make lives for themselves. We need to parent with character in mind so they will be successful when that day arrives.

I remember the extended battle my parents had with one of my sisters over her messy room. She couldn't keep it clean for more than a few minutes before a tornado of activity would sweep through her room, and the floor was once again cluttered. One day I overheard my parents saying to her, "We are no longer going to argue with you about your room. Just keep the door closed so no one has to see it. From now on, we'll just focus our energy on praying for your future husband. Lord, help him!" Today she is a mother of three and married to a pastor in Sacramento, California. Her home is not immaculate, but you will not find another woman with stronger character. My parents chose to major on the majors and minor on the minors. My wife and I have chosen the same course of parenting.

I started a practice with our first-born that I've continued to use to this day for all three girls: When teaching character lessons, I began mentally adding ten years to her age. When she was two years old, I thought ahead to how I wanted her to behave at age twelve. There are plenty of similarities between the ages of two and twelve. Two-year-olds are naturally egotistical, sin-filled creatures who only think of themselves. For two-year-olds, life is all about getting what they want: food, toys, exploring under the kitchen sink, more food, yelling "That's mine!"

and then throwing a Bobby Knight-style tantrum if they don't get their way.

Twelve-year-olds are no different! These preteen creatures are also self-centered, sin-filled, and selfish to the core. In addition to this, their bodies have already started the transformation into adolescence. They are on the verge of hormonal hurricanes that have the potential to wreak havoc in your home if allowed to go unchecked. I've been a pastor to enough junior high students to know that their entire world revolves around getting their way and reacting to how they think they are perceived by others. Their world is in fact quite small, and they firmly believe that they are at its center during this period of their development.

As I looked at my darling but defiant two-year-old, I had a decision to make: Do I begin teaching her character now, or do I wait for another day (or year)? Mentally adding ten years to her age forced me to ask myself an important question: Do I want her acting this way when she is twelve? If I allow pouting and defiance of authority now and call it cute, I am asking for big-time trouble down the road. If I choose to let her disobey her mother and rationalize to myself, "She's only two," I'll be setting up a major confrontation later. Selfish disobedience isn't cute at two, and it's downright frightening at twelve.

We continued to use this parenting tool throughout the next several years with each of our girls. When they were five years old, we focused on the way they talked to and treated their sisters, because we wanted them to be friends when they were 15. When they were eight, we began giving them the decision-making tools that they would need when they turned 18. When Ashley was 15, I began talking to her about the character qualities to look for in a future husband, knowing that the odds of her being married at 25 are relatively high. I can still see her giving me this look that said, "Husband? Dad, I haven't even been asked out on a date yet!" Now that she is approaching 18, we've been talking about her being a mom some day, and all that mothering will entail.

Why do we do this? Because ten years flies by so incredibly fast! This simple tool helps us keep in mind what we as parents are called to do: Prepare our kids for life beyond the walls of our house. The one-word name for this is *character!*

When your children are old enough to leave your home and begin life on their own, they will either fly or fail. They will either soar with confidence or squander precious years in futility. Redeem the time while they are still in your home. Character is king. Teach it. Model it. Reinforce it. We need to love our children enough to give them the necessary nourishment that character provides.

Proper Temperature
The third ingredient for necessary nutrition in a healthy home is having the proper emotional temperature. It has been said that the wife/mother sets the thermostat in the home. Maybe you've heard the saying, "If mama ain't happy, then nobody's happy!" There is a lot of truth in this statement, but I'm not saying that the father plays no part in the temperature in the home. He does. In fact, both parents have a role in establishing the emotional environment in their home.

King Lemuel gives an indication of the temperature his wife set in his home when he says,

> *"She opens her arms to the poor and extends her hands to the needy. She is clothed with strength and dignity; she can laugh at the days to come. She speaks wisdom, and faithful instruction is on her tongue. She watches over the affairs of her household and does not eat the bread of idleness. Her children arise and call her blessed; her husband also, and he praises her." (Proverbs 31:20, 25-28)*

This passage gives us several indicators of the climate of behavior in this home: care for others, dignity, laughter, wisdom, and plenty of praise. He is describing a very pleasant and happy household. Just as physical temperature is a crucial factor in a greenhouse, having the right emotional temperature in a home is necessary for health and growth for all who live under its roof.

I believe that the proper home temperature is one that is emotionally predictable and positive. Everyone should pretty much know what he or she is going to get when they come home. In an unpredictable home you might hear, "I don't know how Dad will be today" or "I hope Mom isn't in one of her moods again." A positive home is a home where encouragement and praise abound.

Here are a few indicators to determine if you're creating the right emotional environment in your home: Do your children ask to have their friends over? Do they look forward to going home? Do *you* want to go home?

I remember a youth group trip to Montana, 15 hours away from our church in Washington where I ministered as a young youth pastor. It was a 10-day ministry trip where our students woke up at 5:30 a.m. every morning and went to sleep at midnight. When we returned home, we were all completely exhausted but satisfied from a successful trip. Before I let them get off the bus, I stood and told my students how proud I was of them. After giving some departing instructions, I said teasingly, "I love you, now go home!"

They all stumbled off the bus except Amy, who began to cry. After everyone was off the bus, I asked her why she was crying. She said, "I don't want to go home." While most of my students were receiving welcoming hugs from their parents in the church parking lot, Amy's father stayed in the truck while she loaded up all of her gear. As soon as she got into the cab, he began to yell at her. I found out later that he was mad because the bus was late. After a 15-hour bus ride home, yes, we were a little later than anticipated, but only 15 *minutes* late! You can probably make some good guesses about the temperature in Amy's home.

Unhealthy temperatures in a home can come in various forms, but the primary ones are emotional and psychological. Emotionally unhealthy homes are evident when one or more family members exhibit outbursts of anger, bitterness and resentment, moodiness, an unforgiving spirit, or emotional disengagement. Psychological issues affect home environments when subtle and not-so-subtle messages are sent that one must be perfect (or close to it) in order to be genuinely loved and accepted. Other kinds of psychologically out-of-balance temperatures include favoritism, broken promises, guilt trips, and unfair comparisons. Unhealthy homes with emotional and psychological issues have thermostats that are inconsistent and unpredictable. This can leave children (and parents!) insecure about love and acceptance in ways that can affect them for the rest of their lives.

When a home has a regular temperature that is too hot, you will find angry words, strife, arguments, and drama. When it is too cold, you will find a lack of communication, distant relationships, awkwardness, and isolation.

In a healthy home with the proper temperature, you will find laughter, love, acceptance, fun, hugging, sharing, listening, caring, and a regular dose of healthy teasing. For the most part, the thermostat in a healthy home has a consistent temperature. All those who live in this home will thrive under these conditions of nourishment.

Spiritual Atmosphere
The fourth ingredient necessary for nourishment in a healthy home is a spiritual atmosphere. King Lemuel closes the chapter with a final beautiful compliment to his wife:

> "Many women do noble things, but you surpass them all. Charm is deceptive, and beauty is fleeting; but a

woman who fears the Lord is to be praised." (Proverbs 31:29-30)

Having a spiritual atmosphere in the home doesn't mean that the family Bible is sitting on the coffee table and regularly dusted. Nor does it mean finding a Bible verse and mounting it on a wall, or sticking a "Jesus Saves" magnet on the refrigerator. Instead, a home with a spiritual atmosphere is a home where God is feared. I'm not talking about "fearing" in the common meaning of "being scared", but in its definition of "being reverent and showing honor." We should strive for a home where God and the things of God are highly respected. This is a home that has regular conversations about God, the Bible, morality, and what God would want us to do. It is a home where a tone of thankfulness is fostered and the things of God are honored. This is a home where spiritual matters are not relegated to a Sunday morning church experience.

As soon as our girls were old enough to communicate and express themselves, my wife and I started teaching them to pray. They were not old enough to understand the theological implications of grace, mercy, and the sacrificial atonement. But they were old enough to tell God all the things they were thankful for. I can still recall one of Kailey's first conversations with God. She said, with her hands tightly folded, "Dear Jesus, I'm thankful for my doggie, for my mommy, for my cereal, and all the animals in the world. Amen!" We wanted to set the stage early on for our girls to realize that God was important in our house.

It may come as a shock to you, but our family doesn't have regular "family devotions" together. I may be a pastor, but that doesn't mean I descend from the stairs every morning wearing priestly robes, holding a Bible in one hand and an incense candle in the other, while singing an ancient Celtic hymn as a call for family devotions. That may work for you, but that is not us!

There have been times that we've read stories that tied into Advent during the Christmas season, and other times where we focused on a different character trait every month. But for the most part, regular and organized family devotions are rare for us, and we have chosen instead to weave those important lessons into our daily life.

When Ashley was in junior high, I spent some time helping her with apologetics – that is, teaching her some key elements about Christianity and how to defend her beliefs. Candy also spent one-on-one time teaching her how to study the Bible for herself. My wife continued this pattern with our other two girls when they reached that age as well. (We have listed what we used in the resource section in the back of the book if you would like to try any of these resources with your own family.)

Our girls have grown up knowing that God is central to our home. He is constantly in our conversations, prayers, questions, and debates. He is Who we go to in prayer every night together as a family. As parents, we are always looking for teachable moments to ask our girls questions about God and His Word, in order to find out how they're processing what they learn about Him and to hear what they're thinking. Our faith is relational, not a ritual, and our girls have caught it. I now see them spending time in God's Word in their rooms on their own. It shows up on their Facebook pages all the time. God is a part of the fabric of their lives, because God is central in our home.

Too many pastors' kids abandon the church as adults because Christianity became artificial and unauthentic at home. They become disillusioned and end up discarding God and the things of God when they grow older. From the very beginning, Candy and I have attempted to counter this trend. The fact of the matter is that there are no guarantees. Every one of our children is a moral free agent with the ability to choose her own course with God. So far, though, the signs are looking positive that each one of our girls is developing an authentic faith of her own.

The kitchen is an essential part of every home. It has the opportunity to provide nourishment to all who live under its roof. Make sure the blueprints for this room will establish a successful place for good nourishment for your family.

Small Group Questions:

Marriage:
1. Describe the health of the marriage in your home.

2. Is your marriage one that will nurture your children to good relational health in their future? If not, what needs to be changed?

3. What kind of marital blueprint will you pass on to your children?

Character:
1. Describe the value of character in your home.

2. Add ten years to the age of each of your children. What do you need to teach them today in order to prepare them for life at that age?

3. What character traits need to be strengthened in your home? What character traits need to be strengthened in your life?

Temperature:
1. Describe the emotional temperature in your home. Does it help make your home a healthy place to grow?

2. Do your children ask to have their friends over? Do they look forward to going home? Do *you* want to go home?

3. How are encouragement and praise evident in your home? How often are encouragement and praise demonstrated in your home?

Spiritual Atmosphere:
1. How often is God brought up in the everyday conversations in your home?

2. How often do you pray as a family?

3. What needs to be changed or rearranged in order for you to begin praying together?

"If you bungle raising your children, I don't think whatever else you do matters very much."
Jacqueline Kennedy Onassis

Chapter Two
The Kids' Room: Parenting with Purpose

Emergency room doctors have the best stories! They see just about everything. Several years back I heard a true story from the ER in Nicholasville, Kentucky. The doctor was treating a man who had been in an automobile accident and, rather than the whiplash or bruised ribs you might expect, he was suffering from angry red burn marks around his neck. The doctor was understandably curious about what had happened. The story went something like this.

> "My wife and I were sittin' on our front porch talkin' about the new shock collar we just got for our dog. We were wonderin' how far that shock collar zapper would reach. I said to my wife, 'Honey, I'm gonna put this on and get in the car. I'm gonna give you the zapper and I'm gonna back the car out and see how far this thing works. When I honk, you zap!'"

> Here's what happened. He put the shock collar around his neck, gave her the zapper, and backed the car out of the yard. He drove down the road a ways and honked – and sure enough, she zapped. It just about knocked him unconscious, and he started swerving all over the road. What his wife couldn't see from the front porch was that another car was coming up the hill. Seeing a car in his lane

and coming right at him, the other driver did exactly what any of us would do: He honked his horn! Every time the car swerved toward him, he honked again. And every time the wife heard the horn, well, you guessed it … she kept right on zapping. (Story told by Erwin McManus at Willow Creek Conference – 2005)

I've seen some parents swerving all over the road, completely clueless when it comes to raising their children. They have no idea how to love, discipline, or nurture their kids. These parents tend to make decisions based on the emotion of the moment. For many of these people, their poor parenting skills are a result of flying blind as parents, having never witnessed or experienced what healthy parenting should look like.

The next blueprint in our Dream House is for the kids' room. This room is different from all the other rooms in the house. It usually has its own unique color scheme, often blue for the boys and pink for the girls. (Or if your girls are like mine, it might be purple or bright yellow, decorated with dozens of snapshots of friends and pictures of the Eiffel Tower, or full of Seattle Mariners memorabilia!) The kids' room, in our metaphor, represents the stage of life in which children are still moldable and pliable. Their whole life is in front of them. It's in this "room" of their life that their little personalities begin to emerge.

Our family loves to watch our home movies from the years when the girls were little. We laugh together at the funny little ways they used to talk, how they consistently butchered our family's last name, and the way they rolled the "r" in their words. I also love looking back at the enthusiasm and delight they displayed at life's simplest things – ice cream, flowers, animals, presents, and snow could all make them giddy with excitement. Candy and I were completely fine with them being naïve and innocent at this age, knowing that the harshness of life would eventually catch up to them. It's this period – life in the kids' room – where time flies much too quickly for many parents.

This is why parents must have purpose in their parenting. They must know what they want to teach, inspire, and pass on to their children at this tender age – and just as importantly, they need to know how to do it. This time of instinctive openness to parental guidance only comes once, and then it is gone.

Sadly, there are parents who have little to no actual purpose in their parenting. From their self-centered perspective, their children are just a byproduct of passionate sex, and the main thing they want now is for the "little brats" to just stay out of their hair. These parents don't want to be bothered with the responsibilities that come with raising healthy children. These are the children who are often ignored, abandoned, neglected, and/or abused.

Other parents *do* have a purpose in their parenting, but it is selfish and often immature. These parents are trying to relive their own lives in and through their children. Although they appear on the surface to mean well, in reality they are manipulating situations or relationships so that their children can have what they feel was lacking in their own lives. If they didn't date, you can bet their kids are going to date. These kids are often pushed to begin dating much too soon, with predictably disastrous results. If the parent wasn't very athletic as a child, their kids are going to start early in every sports league possible. These parents are easy to spot at kids' sporting events – they're the ones screaming at the umpires, the coaches, and the kids, acting like their four-year-old is one step away from getting that elusive college scholarship. These children frequently grow up from arrogant children into arrogant adults after being told how great they are for their whole lives; or, at the opposite extreme, they can be deeply insecure due to a sense of never being good enough to please their parents.

Then there are parents whose purpose in parenting is simply vague. They love their kids, they really do. They just struggle to show it. They know they should teach their children some not-entirely-defined "stuff" to help them function in life, but there is no real effort or game plan to their parenting. These parents tend to do the bare minimum in raising their children. These homes feel empty and are often quiet. There are no real fights or arguments, but the pulse of love and real living are barely above a coma state.

One of our essential purposes as parents is to teach our children basic life skills. In early childhood, we need to teach our children to walk, to be potty trained, and to brush their teeth. They also need to learn how to say "please", "thank you" and "I'm sorry." The alphabet and numbers are must-haves, along with the ability to color inside the lines. (Unless, of course, you're one of those artistic and creative parents who believe that coloring outside the lines is a vital part of healthy self-expression!) We also need to teach them to read and write, tie their shoes, answer the phone, ride a bike, never talk to strangers, put their dishes in the sink, and of course, "Clean your room!"

(In my house, we added a few "necessary" skills to this list - piano lessons were required by their mother, so I balanced it out by teaching my girls how to properly throw a spiral, along with the intricacies of the two-deep zone in football.)

All of these are necessary life skills that will help our children to become successful in the next stage of life. But these are just the basic, minimal requirements that we as parents must pass along to our kids. There is a greater purpose for lifelong success that parents must have in mind at all times. We must parent with a *godly* purpose. Let me encourage you with these four important elements for the blueprint of the kids' room.

Follow Me as I Follow God

Deuteronomy 6 tells us *why* we should parent with a godly purpose, and then it tells us how. Let's begin with the *why*. The rebar of this passage is basically this:

> *"These are the commands, decrees and laws the Lord your*
> *God directed me to teach you...so that you, your children,*
> *and their children... may enjoy long life...so that it may*
> *go well with you and that you may increase greatly."*
> *(Deuteronomy 6:1-3)*

This is a pretty persuasive *why*! Breaking it down, we find this essential meaning: "Obey these commands, and you and your family will be successful and enjoy a long life." Sign me up today! What parent wouldn't want this?

What commands, decrees, and laws is Moses referring to? None other than the Ten Commandments, found in the previous chapter! We've all seen news reports in recent years where these ancient passages have been removed from the public square and our public schools. One court case banned the posting of the Ten Commandments in the classroom, explaining their decision with this statement in the final opinion on the case: "If the posted copies of the Ten Commandments are to have any effect at all, it will be to induce the schoolchildren to read, meditate upon, perhaps to venerate and obey, the Commandments."[1] And this wasn't just a minor ruling in a small court – this was the U.S. Supreme Court! Of all the problems our schools are facing today with violence, drugs, rape, sexting, and an increasing number of teachers who are having sex with their students, hiding the Ten Commandments from our kids should be the least of our worries.

When was the last time you read the Ten Commandments? I don't know about you, but I sure wouldn't call them radical or extreme! We'll talk more about them in Chapter Four, but for now, the important thing to know is that the Ten Commandments are God's blueprint for how to love God and live with people. Their worldview teaches us that life is bigger than ourselves. Imprinting this blueprint on our children's hearts is at the center of our true purpose as parents. Learning these principles while they are still young and impressionable will save our children from the life of chaos and confusion that results from a life lived apart from God.

This important transfer of information and morality starts with the parents. We must communicate to our children in word and deed: "Follow me as I follow God." Saying, "Do as I say, not as I do" is foolishness and a sure-fire plan for failure.

Live It!

Deuteronomy 6 also clearly lays out *how* we are to parent with a godly purpose:

> *"Love the Lord your God with all your heart and with all your soul and with all your strength. These commandments that I give you today are to be upon your hearts. Impress them on your children." (Deuteronomy 6:5-7a)*

If we are going to parent with a godly purpose and call our children to "follow me as I follow God," then we must live this truth, and live it passionately! God starts with us as parents when He says that we are to love Him with "*all* your heart and with *all* your soul and with *all* your strength" (emphasis added). This describes parents whose entire lives are characterized by a passionate and personal pursuit of God. You can't fake this. It must be real, or you will be exposed.

As we live this out in our own lives, God commands us to impress this passion for Him onto our children. The Hebrew word *shanan*, translated here as "impress", has two meanings in the original language. The first meaning, implied in this passage, is "to sharpen." Sharpening a sword requires regular application with the sharpening stone. You couldn't just take a halfhearted swipe at the blade with a whetstone every now and then and expect it to stay sharp. No, it needs consistent maintenance for it to become an effective instrument.

From my earliest memories, my parents took my siblings and me to church every Sunday. We were not of a voting age so, like clockwork, we attended. They were sharpening the sword every weekend.

One Sunday morning I realized that if I went to church, I would miss an important football game on TV. Since VCRs and DVRs had not yet been invented, all I could do was use my best dramatic skills to pretend that I was sick so I could stay home and catch the game. My father looked at me suspiciously, but agreed to let me stay home. When he closed my bedroom door, I pumped my arm in victory. *Yes!* I'd pulled it off! I waited until I was sure my family had left for church, and then ran downstairs, only to discover that I just might end up being sick after all. A wave of nausea hit me when I saw that my dad had removed the power cord to the television! I can still hear him saying, "If you are too sick to go to church, then you are too sick to watch TV." The sword of my heart got pounded on that morning.

I remember another Sunday morning where I was overwhelmed by what I saw as the monotony of church in general, and hymns in particular. In an agony of boredom, a thought struck me – "I wonder if my dad is into this, or if he's as bored as I am?" I turned in my metal folding chair and looked up at my father. My dad was hard of hearing in one ear, and it made him sound horrible when he attempted to sing. But there he was, singing his heart out. I remember thinking to myself, "If he's into this, then I will be too." I truly believed that if my father was bored with this whole Jesus thing, then it was all the excuse I needed to do the same – but if it was important to him, then it'd better be important to me, too. The sword got a little sharper that day.

In verse seven, the Hebrew word for *impress* can also be translated "to whet." This means "to excite or stimulate," as seen in the English phrase "to whet your appetite." Parents whet their children's appetites all the time, for all kinds of things, whether we're conscious of it or not! The things we are passionate about, the activities that we give our time and energy to, are the things we teach our children to value.

I bleed the color red – San Francisco 49er red. Why? Easy – it was my dad's favorite team! He didn't have to sit me down and give a point-by-point explanation of why 1970's-era Niners stars John Brodie and Gene Washington were worth following. He whetted my appetite for the game just by jumping up and down and cheering when the 49ers scored a touchdown. My passion later grew as I got older and followed Joe Montana and Jerry Rice, and it continues with me to this day no matter how good (or bad!) my team is. Now two of my girls (I am praying for Kailey to get her heart right with Jesus) are huge 49er fans. Why? Kids usually end up adopting the passions of their parents.

God knows this. He knows that the most powerful influence in a child's life is his parents. That is why God starts with Mom and Dad. God knows that our kids will, in many cases, pick up on the things that catch our attention. Church programs have plenty to offer, don't get me wrong – but God didn't point to a church program, He pointed to parents. God designed the family to be the *primary* place where faith is nurtured and caught. While church programs are a great side dish, parents offer the main course for a relationship with God to flourish.

Communicate It!

We talk about the things that are important to us. If you're into politics, you'll find a way to bring up politics in a conversation. If you're into hunting, the first sign of wildlife (including road kill) is an excuse to mention the start of hunting season. If you're passionate about shopping, you'll find yourself casually dropping the latest sale at the mall into conversation. You've seen this with first-time grandparents. You could be in a conversation about the Middle East peace process and they stop and say, "That reminds me, have you seen a picture of my grandbaby?" You offer a polite smile and feign interest, all the while mentally struggling to connect the dots between their grandchild and the Golan Heights. To them, the connection doesn't matter. Why? Our passions spill over. We can't help ourselves.

Deuteronomy 6 also lets us know *when* we should communicate to our children about God and the things of God. It says,

> *"Impress them on your children. Talk about them when you sit at home and when you walk along the road, when you lie down and when you get up." (Deuteronomy 6:7)*

In our home, Candy's and my love for God spills over, all the time. Sometimes it's unintentional. Other times, it's *very* intentional. We talk about God in the kitchen, before bed, after school, while driving in the car, and even while we're watching television. As life flows, our communication about God flows. Beyond the unplanned everyday conversations, here are some examples of instances where we've taken intentional steps to communicate the things of God to our girls:

- **Questions.** At random times, I will call out, "*Questions!*" My girls know this is their cue for a time when they can ask me any question about my life, their mom, God, the Bible, or life in general. When they were young, I would do this as I was tucking them into bed. Later, I did this while cruising around Kitsap County as the family taxi driver. I've had questions that range from the innocent and cute to the bizarre. It's a simple opportunity for me to intertwine a few words about God and His plan for our lives into my answers. It also communicates to my kids that it is safe to ask any question.

- **The Daddy Tape.** On a snowy day when Ashley was young, I recorded a cassette tape (remember those?) filled with "Daddy stories." I gave my own weird version of "Goldilocks and the Three Bears" that I knew would make her laugh. I told Bible stories from Adam and Eve to David and his mighty men. I'd insert funny side stories about David stopping at McDonald's for a cheeseburger, just so she'd cry out, "Daddy, *that's* not in the Bible!" I also told adventure stories from when I was a young boy – stories about trusting my father, obedience, and faith. This Daddy Tape was a great tool that allowed me to creatively weave in my love for God and how important it is to trust Him. All the girls ended up listening to it so many times that the cassette tape stretched out until I sounded like a tired James Earl Jones.

- **Character Traits**. As I mentioned in the last chapter, Candy and I did a series of month-long character lessons with the girls when they were young. We covered truthfulness, initiative, responsibility, thoughtfulness, diligence, and other positive traits. We used a wonderful resource called *Achieving True Success: How to Build Character as a Family*. This resource provided a personal story, memory verses, and an animal from nature that demonstrated each character trait. My girls loved the illustrations and still remember these principles.

- **Keys for Kids.** Candy used this Walk Thru the Bible resource with Holly and Kailey. She'd sit down with the girls in the morning and read the short story, and then the girls would talk about it and answer the provided questions. Both girls remember lessons from this little booklet to this day, and Kailey used it years later to help a friend through a difficult time.

- *Heaven for Kids.* One summer, while Ashley was in India on a mission's trip, we took this book (written by Randy Alcorn) with us on vacation. Every night of the trip, Holly and Kailey each got to select two questions from the table of contents concerning heaven. I then read the answer from Alcorn's book. When Kailey asked the question "Will there be animals in heaven?" the tears began to well up in her eyes. After I read the answer, the floodgates opened. Earlier in the summer, we'd had to put down our dog, Maddie, because she had attacked Kailey for no apparent reason. Kailey loved that dog, and she hadn't yet fully mourned the loss. We found out that she was quietly blaming herself for Maddie's death. She thought she had done something wrong to cause this unprovoked attack. This gave Candy and me the opportunity to walk her through this pain and provide answers for her tender heart.

In our home, Christianity isn't confined to being a Sunday-only religious experience. It is an everyday lifestyle throughout the week. As parents, our passions will spill over into our children's minds and hearts. It *will* happen. It can't be helped! In every home, intentionally or not, parents are communicating what they are passionate about. Most likely, our children will catch our passion and adopt it as their own. What's spilling over in your home?

Repeat It!

Repetition is the first law of learning. In sports and military training, athletes and soldiers execute the same drills over and over again until muscle memory kicks in and the action becomes instinctive. In order for me to memorize anything, I have to write the whole thing down and say it out loud, repeating it over and over again until it sticks. The same is true for handing down our passions to our children. God continues His instructions to parents in this passage:

> *"Tie them as symbols on your hands and bind them on your foreheads. Write them on the door frames of your houses and on your gates." (Deuteronomy 6:8-9)*

By the time of Christ, religious leaders in Israel had developed a tradition of taking this passage completely literally, and ended up missing the whole point. They made little boxes, called phylacteries, which contained passages of the Law written in tiny letters on miniature scrolls. They would affix the boxes to the doorpost of every door, and they wore similar items on their heads and arms to symbolize the instruction of this passage. Since they neglected to teach the true message of God's instruction to their children, over time the phylacteries became a religious exercise that was without meaning.

Whether it is taught in vision statements, values, traditions, or stories, we will forget what we do not repeat. In this passage, God is stressing the point of repetition, not for repetition's sake, but as a tool to learn what is truly important.

At every stage of my girls' lives, I want them to hear over and over, "I love God! I love your mother, and I love you." If it is repeated enough, they will absorb it into every part of their hearts and minds. Over time, this truth will be impressed upon them so thoroughly that it will become instinctive to them: "My dad loves God, loves my mother, and loves me!"

The Kids' Room in this Dream House is vitally important because children are like wet cement in these early years. What is impressed on them at this age will last a lifetime. This foundation will determine what can be built in later stages in their lives.

Again, there are no guarantees because they are moral free agents, but the likelihood of success increases significantly when the Kids' Room is properly, intentionally prepared with a godly purpose. Parents who tell their children to "Follow me as I follow God" may not do everything perfectly, but if they live it, communicate it, and repeat it to their children, these parents will have few regrets when life really begins to hit their children in the next stage of development – the teenage years!

Small Group Questions:

1. Did your parents seem to have a purpose behind their parenting? How would you describe the way they raised you?

2. Are you following Deuteronomy 6:5-7? If so, how?

3. How are you "impressing" your love for God on the hearts of your children?

4. What are you passionate about in life? Are your children mimicking these passions? If so, how?

5. Is God relegated to a church experience, or is He part of your everyday lifestyle? What does this choice communicate to your children?

"Few things are more satisfying than to see your children have teenagers of their own."
Doug Larson

Chapter Three
The Teenagers' Room: Vital Information

Teenagers get a bad rap. I've worked with thousands of teenagers over the course of 20 years as a youth pastor, and I believe this now even more than when I started out. Some people think we can just simplify things by giving teenagers four basic instructions: "Clean your room, don't wear that, change your attitude, and what part of 'no' do you not understand?" Sorry, it's not that simple! Not even close.

Some joke that Mark Twain was right on the money when he reportedly said, "When a child turns 13, put them in a barrel and feed them through the knot hole. When they turn 16, plug up the hole!"

Let me be clear: *God loves teenagers!* The Bible is full of significant characters who were teenagers – Joseph, Joshua, David, Jonathan, Daniel, and Mary. Other possible teenagers were Queen Esther and the disciples of Jesus, except for Peter. God loves teenagers because they are passionate about what matters to them, enthusiastically loyal (sometimes to a fault), and often willing to take extreme risks in demonstrating their faith in God.

In spite of this, the teenage years often scare many parents. For some, it brings back memories of their own adolescent years. They remember all too well the impulsive, unwise, or downright crazy choices they made, and they're paralyzed by the fear that their son or daughter will make the same mistakes. They check out of their parenting responsibilities, dropping their kids off at one youth group event and sports practice after another, hoping that the church staff and coaches will parent their children for them. Other parents try to balance out their own wild teen years by raising their children within an extensive set of rules and regulations – the default answer to any request is "no", and open discussion with their children is rare. Still others react to a strict upbringing by letting the pendulum swing in the opposite direction – they raise their children with so little guidance and discipline that their children stray over unmarked boundaries and get into every kind of trouble. Any one of these extreme approaches has the potential to cause serious unintended harm to the parent-teenager relationship far into the future.

On the other hand, even parents without a lot of baggage from their past may also struggle with fear when their child reaches the teenage years. This fear is a result of seeing too many crash-and-burn examples from the evening news, the never-ending parade of burned-out teenagers in our pop culture, or simply from personal friends who have had a difficult time with their own teenagers. These parents worry that their child will become one of the sad statistics that result in pain and heartache for everyone involved.

Believe me, as a youth pastor and dad of two teenagers, I understand the fear that accompanies the adolescent years! Many times I have counseled parents that the teenage years are similar to being on a zip line. If you've never seen one of these, imagine a cable attached between two points (maybe a couple of trees in the woods with a cleared space and a downward slope between them), and a harness attached to the cable on a pulley. You (or more likely your 14-year-old, egged on by the rest of his friends) strap yourself in, grab the hand grips, and push off, sailing down the hill on the pulley until you come to the other end with a serious case of windblown hair and your heart pounding with adrenaline. That's the summer camp version. But the parenting version of the zip line goes across the 1,000-foot-deep canyon between childhood and adulthood, with all manner of known and unknown risks in the dark chasm below.

The dangers in the canyon below are real. In my role as a youth pastor, I've had to rappel down into this canyon with parents and face the tragic results of students who got involved in drugs and alcohol abuse. Other students, ignoring repeated warnings and advice, chose to engage in premarital sex, with some reaping the consequences of a teen pregnancy. Other teenagers became so overwhelmed with the pressures that accompany adolescence that they developed eating disorders or began to physically cut themselves in an effort to release their inner pain. I've also sat with brokenhearted parents in hospital rooms at the bedsides of teenagers who attempted suicide, the ultimate escape from the hurts and stresses of these often difficult years.

I vividly remember receiving a phone call early one morning from the distraught mother of a girl in my youth group. She pleaded for me to come to their house immediately. When I arrived, I found the parents at a complete loss as to why their daughter was curled into the fetal position on her bed, crying and refusing to come out of her room. I sat with these loving parents as they held their daughter, and through sobs and tears she revealed to us that she had been date raped on the night of her senior prom.

Don't let these true stories paralyze you if you have a teenager or a child entering adolescence. I had hundreds and hundreds of students, by far the majority, whose worst experience as a teenager was battling the typical ebb and flow of emotions, crashing hormones, zits, and friendship dramas. Those things are absolutely normal during these turbulent teenage years. One by one most of my students crossed over the adolescent canyon without any major issues or life-altering crises.

Parents, listen carefully: Don't send your teenager across the canyon on the zip line by themselves! You can't just send them off with a cheerful wave and an attitude that communicates, "I'll meet you on the other side!" Too many parents disengage during these teenage years, but it is the worst possible time to do this. Don't be fooled into believing that when your child was younger they needed you more, and that they don't need you as much now that they're a teenager. In fact, they need you now more than ever. What they need, and how they need you, just looks different now.

Parents, buckle up, attach your harness to the cable, and hold on for the ride. They've got a long journey ahead, and you need to go *with* them.

Don't get me wrong – I'm not implying that you need to become a Helicopter Parent. You've seen them – always hovering, controlling, manipulating, and not allowing room for their teenager to breathe. They're the ones who say to their 15-year-old daughter, "I saw you talking with that boy. Anything you say can and will be held against you in the court of Mom!"

Instead, I'm suggesting that parents need to be engaged enough to pass on to their teenager some absolutely vital information as they make the trip across this adolescent canyon. They'll spend these years surrounded by the sound of confusing and competing messages, and they need to have a parent who is reinforcing them with information that is critical for success in their turbulent teenage years. Doing so will make a world of difference in their lives and in your family!

Vital information

Your child needs to know a few crucial things for the years ahead. It's the same information she needed when she was a little girl, and she'll continue to need to hear it even when she's grown up. But it is absolutely critical that teenagers have regular reminders of this vital information when they are going through the most traumatic change in their lives. Therefore, your communication of these principles cannot be vague, incomplete, or insincere. It must be simple, straightforward, and genuine, because the teenage years can be a time where everything seems to be upside down. Their priorities change, their values become more complex as they mature, and what appeared to be so simple as a child ("Always tell Mommy the truth") is now more complicated ("Be loyal to your friends, and *never* rat them out to your parents").

I know adults who continue to struggle because they didn't receive this support from their parents while they were teenagers. These adults love God, they're working hard, and some of them are very successful by all outward appearances. But inside, they are still floundering because they didn't receive a regular dose of this vital information when they were younger.

What is this information that is so essential for our children? In its simplest form, it is this: Your child needs to know that you love him, that you're proud of him, and that you notice what he does well. We find examples of this principle on two different occasions in the gospel of Matthew. In both instances, the voice of God the Father comes forth from the realms of heaven, communicating these important concepts to His Son in a powerful and poignant way.

In Matthew 3, on the verge of beginning His earthly ministry and just prior to facing incredible temptation in the wilderness, Jesus is baptized. Matthew writes,

> "As soon as Jesus was baptized, he went up out of the water. At that moment heaven was opened, and he saw the Spirit of God descending like a dove and lighting on him. And a voice from heaven said, 'This is my Son, whom I love; with him I am well pleased.'" (Matthew 3:16-17)

Did you catch it? Do you see how God values His Son so highly, and makes sure He communicates it clearly at this key moment?

The second time we see this vital information coming from God the Father is in Matthew 17. Jesus has taken Peter, James, and John with Him to the top of a high mountain, and something supernatural takes place. Jesus is transfigured, meaning that He began to take on His heavenly appearance, right there in front of them. And as if that wasn't astounding enough, Moses and Elijah show up! These three young men are utterly amazed at what they're seeing. Two of the disciples were smart enough to keep their mouths shut ... and then there's Peter. He couldn't contain himself, and started going on about his great new idea of a special building project to honor Jesus, Moses, and Elijah. It made perfect sense to him to preserve this majestic moment with a monument to mark the occasion, and Peter, ever practical, was ready to start building *right now.* He was on a roll until God the Father interrupts him mid-sentence. (It's never a good sign when you are interrupted by God.) Matthew writes:

> *"While he was speaking, a bright cloud enveloped them, and a voice from the cloud said, 'This is my Son, whom I love; with him I am well pleased. Listen to him!' When the disciples heard this, they fell facedown to the ground, terrified. But Jesus came and touched them. 'Get up,' he said. 'Don't be afraid.' When they looked up, they saw no one except Jesus." (Matthew 17:5-8)*

After God finished speaking, the moment was over. I can imagine the four of them descending the mountain, with James and John giving Peter a look and shaking their heads. I can hear Peter protesting, "What? I thought it was a good idea, okay?" I can see John shaking his head while James mumbles to himself, "Idiot!" Even with Peter's impulsive words of the moment, though, God's statement still must have echoed in their heads.

God the Father could have said so many different things in these times when he chose to speak out loud to Jesus in front of other people. He could have said, "Believe him!" "The Messiah has come!" "Trust in Jesus", or "I'm coming back soon and boy, am I ticked!" Of all the things he could have said, God didn't say anything like this. Instead, God told Jesus and those with him the same simple things we all need to hear – "I love you. I'm proud of you. You're doing well."

But why did God say what He said? Was Jesus insecure? No! Did Jesus forget or doubt the love of God the Father? No! Was God struggling with heavenly empty nest syndrome? Absolutely not. We will probably never fully understand all the layers of meaning in God's communication with His Son, but I believe we can learn from it.

"I love you!"

The first piece of vital information consists of the three most powerful words in any human language: "I love you" This simple phrase holds great power in the lives of children, teenagers, and adults alike. It is oxygen to our souls, energy to our emotions, and fuel for our relationships. The first thing God the Father declares to Jesus is His love for Him. Incredible.

In 2003, a teen chick flick came out called *What a Girl Wants*. The movie previews gave the impression that what a girl wants is shopping, a boyfriend, and her freedom, but the real story was much deeper. Amanda Bynes stars as Daphne, a teenager whose mother left her father before she was born. She grows up with a deep desire to meet her father, to know him and be known by him. She and her mother work for a wedding planner, and as she waits tables at the receptions, she hears her mom sing for countless father-daughter dances. Her heart aches for the father she has never met, wishing to have this experience with him.

When Daphne discovers that her father is a politician in London, she runs away to find him. When she unexpectedly shows up to meet her father (who was completely unaware of her existence), it doesn't go over well at all. Daphne embarks on a mission to change herself in a desperate attempt to fit into his world and be accepted by him. As their relationship grows, conflict arises with her father's promising career. Daphne returns home, disillusioned and discouraged.

In the final scene, we see Daphne at another wedding listening to her mother sing as the call for the father/daughter dance is announced. Daphne turns away and is surprised to see an unexpected guest walking toward her. While the music plays, her father stumbles to explain why he is there. He has something important he wants to say to her, but he's flustered because he can't seem to find the talking points he wrote during his flight. He stops, looks her in the eyes and says, "What it comes down to is, I love you, Daphne. I'm so sorry. I wouldn't change anything about you." Daphne throws her arms around him and says, "I love you, Dad!" After a precious embrace, her dad asks Daphne for the honor of this dance.[2]

I've seen this movie many times, and every time I watch it, I tear up because of the powerful truth it reveals. This is truly what a teenage girl wants – to know, and to *hear*, that she is loved. Teenage guys need and want to hear that they are loved as well; it just looks a little different with guys than it does with girls. Your son probably won't want to dance, but a quick bear hug or wrestling match may suffice. But don't assume these actions will fully communicate what he needs to *hear* – "I love you, son!"

My father never heard the words "I love you" from his dad. This made it difficult for my dad to express this key truth to his own children. But he fought through the awkwardness of his past, and learned to say it anyway. At first, he simply wrote these powerful words to us in notes or in birthday cards. Later, my father became more comfortable actually saying it out loud. The truth is, I didn't care *how* he told me – what mattered was that he did.

When my girls were young, I made up unique ways to tell each of them that I loved them. It was my way of letting them know that I loved them in a special way apart from their sisters. I'd tell Ashley, "I love you tons!" Holly's phrase evolved to, "I love you goobs, gobs, sniggles, and wiggles." (Don't ask me how it came to be, it just did.) Kailey grew up hearing me tell her, "I love you a whooooole lot, baby!" Although they're older now and seem to have outgrown our silly expressions, I still tell each of them on a daily basis that I love them. Just the other night, out of the blue, my junior-higher kissed me goodnight, and with a twinkle in her eyes she whispered in my ear, "Goobs, gobs, sniggles, and wiggles!" We both knew what she meant.

Think about it – God the Father personally showed us the importance of these words by telling His Son and everyone who listened, "This is my Son, whom I love." Powerful. Meaningful. It is an example parents must follow.

"I am proud of you!"

The second piece of vital information our teenage sons and daughters need to hear is that we are proud of them. God the Father modeled this for us when He communicated in clear and simple terms that He was "well pleased" with Jesus.

Telling your teenager that you are proud of him or her is important. Why? This short phrase communicates acceptance and worth. When our kids are little, this phrase seems to bounce off of them with apparently little to no impact. They can tell that "I'm proud of you" means something good, but I don't believe that they are able at that age to fully comprehend the significance of these words.

With teenagers, it's different. Their world revolves around a desperate need for acceptance and worth. Many parents are at a loss when their once easygoing, happy child suddenly morphs into a sensitive bundle of roller-coaster emotions who insists on wearing That One Shirt at least twice a week. What happened? Hormones, of course. But something else has changed, too: The part of their brain and heart that desperately needs acceptance is fired up and running in high gear. This is why teenagers overreact when they do something stupid, clumsy, or embarrassing. Their fear of rejection skyrockets.

This powerful need for acceptance and worth is one of the reasons gangs hold such a huge appeal for teenagers. Those who live in and around gangs know full well that joining a gang is dangerous and sometimes deadly. They've heard the sirens in the middle of the night and they've seen friends or family members shot. But the pull of the gang is still strong. If you pass their initiation test, you are accepted. You are valued. You are *in*.

Although adolescents can mask it well, deep down in the heart of every teenager is a desire to please their parents. Survey after survey validates this claim. Yes, their friends are important to them, but nothing compares to the powerful pull of their parents. When teenagers find acceptance and worth at home, it will reduce the need for them to engage in a desperate search for it outside the home.

Sarah (not her real name) was in my high school group when I was a high school pastor in Fullerton, California. I could spot her insecurity a mile away. She was a good student and an excellent athlete who raced from one endeavor to the next in search of acceptance, from anybody and everybody. She thought making good grades or being named captain of the softball team would make her parents proud of her. It didn't, or at least she didn't think so. In Sarah's eyes, her parents failed to notice her high grades and rarely came to her softball games because they were so consumed with their impending divorce.

Sarah was lost, confused, and on the verge of quitting school, sports, and even life. You should have seen the look on her face the time I put my arm around her and told her how proud I was of her for something she'd done. It was like a flower opening up to the rays of the sun. Passing this insight on to Sarah's core group leader allowed her leader to shower her with praise and encouragement. Sarah transformed before our eyes from an overly needy and attention-seeking girl to one who quickly grew to be a steady, confident leader in our youth group.

Last week, my Holly attempted to run for 8th grade class president. She didn't win, but you wouldn't have known it by how we reacted when she returned home from school that day. We celebrated! We made sure she understood that we were proud of her for trying when many students won't even attempt something like this, out of fear of failure. The look on her face was unforgettable.

Tell your teenagers often that you are proud of them. Let them know that you "caught them" making a good effort at school, listening to their coach, diving for that ball, being faithful with their piano practice, doing what you asked them to do, having a good attitude even when they're tired – and even more importantly, that you're proud of them simply for who they are.

Your words may appear to bounce off of them and hit the floor with no positive effect, but don't buy their nonchalant response. Deep down, these seeds of encouragement are being implanted in their soul, and they will eventually bear fruit. Over time you'll begin to see a more confident teenager who feels accepted for who they are and for what they do.

"You're good at…"

The third piece of vital information modeled for us was unveiled at the transfiguration when God the Father interrupted Peter with the words, *"Listen to him!"* If God had said this about us in the presence of others, we'd probably never have to worry about our self-esteem again! This phrase says to the listener, "He knows what He's doing! My Son is important! Stop talking and listen to Him!" God was fully aware of what was happening on that mountain top, and He knew that if Peter didn't shut up for a minute, he was going to miss something important.

Parents, do you remember when your children were little, and they were forever trying to get your attention? Whether it was showing off a new trick at the playground or tumbling over and over again on the living room carpet, they'd shout, "Mommy, watch! Watch me!" or "Daddy, let me show you something!"

Now they're teenagers, but deep down, nothing has really changed. On the outside, they may be insisting, "Don't watch me, it's embarrassing!" But on the inside, they're secretly whispering, "I still hope they notice."

Before every athletic game I played in high school, I tried to give the impression that I was confident and ready, fully focused at the task at hand. But that didn't stop me from looking around until I spotted one or both of my parents, making sure I knew exactly where they were sitting in the stands. Throughout the game I'd look out of the corner of my eye to make sure they'd seen the play I had just made. Deep down, I wanted to know they were watching.

Saying "You're good at _____" tells your teenager that you've been watching them. It says, "I notice you! I've seen you in action, and I see something positive in you." It's simple, but powerful and deeply meaningful – more than many parents realize.

Parents cannot pass this vital information along to their kids if they are not watching. Many parents are so consumed with their career, their finances, or their own personal problems that the amazing things that their teenager is doing, big things and little things, go by unseen – unnoticed by the most influential people in their life.

Parents who take notice of their teenagers have the opportunity to become covert seed planters while providing additional doses of needed encouragement as their children grow into adults.

Honest comments like these go a long way:

- "You sure are good with your hands."
- "You can fix just about anything!"
- "You're really good at math. How'd you get so smart?!"
- "You are a hard worker. This character trait will take you far in life!"
- "God has gifted you with musical ability. Be sure to use it for His glory!"
- "Wow! You're so creative, the way you designed that brochure for your class project. Great job."
- "I've noticed that you're a great friend to your friends. I appreciate how you keep being kind to them even when they let you down."
- "You are so reliable and responsible. That's why teachers ask you to do things. They know they can count on you to come through!"

When parents make *honest* comments like these, it tells children that their parents are noticing them. It is also providing their son or daughter extra motivation to continue doing what he or she is doing. All of us need to hear when we're doing things well!

Sometimes teenagers aren't even aware of how their actions are making a positive impact and lasting impression on others. Telling them what they're doing right can make a world of difference both to your teenager and to the people they're affecting.

When I was in high school, my 10-year-old brother Bobby was a first-class nuisance. I called him "my shadow" because every time I turned around he'd ask, "Where are you going? Can I come?" He'd ask this as I was leaving the house to run up to the 7-Eleven, to put gas in my car, or to see my girlfriend. It was the same thing every time: "Where are you going? Can I come?" One day he caught me walking down the hallway in our house. He came running out of his room shouting, "Where are you going?" I said, "To the *bathroom*! Do you *mind*?" To which he replied, "Can I come?" I think I hit him.

One day my mom pulled me aside and told me that I was "such a good older brother," and how much Bobby looked up to me. She told me that he mimicked me because he wanted to be just like me. I was floored. I hadn't really noticed this before – I'd been caught up in his pesky habit of following me around, and I hadn't thought about what it might actually mean. Then my mind quickly replayed the ways he tried to dress like me, walk like me, and talk like me. I still remember her closing comment. She said, "Because he looks up to you so much, you have a great opportunity to influence his life."

My relationship with my brother changed that day. Instead of viewing him as a pest to avoid, I began looking for opportunities to invest in our relationship – inviting him to go places with me and making time to talk with him about girls, friends, God, and life in general. My mother probably didn't realize it at the time, but she tapped into every man's number one need – significance. At 16, I accepted her challenge, and my brother became one of my best friends. Even today, over 30 years later, my mother's "You are a good big brother" echoes in my ears. I am still motivated to keep living up to her challenge.

What happens without this information?

These three pieces of vital information are all about encouragement, which is like oxygen, essential for the life and health of the soul. Without this reinforcement, teenagers struggle to breathe. The apostle Paul reminds fathers in Colossians 3:21,

> "Fathers, do not embitter your children, or they will become discouraged."

The word *embitter* is also translated "exasperate," which means "to frustrate." If our teenagers don't hear these three reminders on a regular basis, they will become frustrated. They may end up being convinced that "No matter what I do, it will never be good enough for my dad!" or "I can never please my mom! Why can't she accept me for who I am?" This will force your teenager to begin searching for love and acceptance elsewhere, often with disastrous and heartbreaking results.

The word *discourage* in this verse means "to lose courage; to lose heart." If teenagers don't hear their parents say, "I love you," "I am proud of you," and "You are good at this," they will go through life wondering if they were loved. They will wonder if they ever were accepted. They will wonder if they are good at anything. These questions have the potential to rattle around in their heart and soul, haunting them for the rest of their lives.

Those who grow up without hearing this vital information from their parents frequently become adults who are hesitant in making decisions and commitments. They lack the self-confidence necessary to try new things or take risks. A little voice is constantly whispering to them that they aren't good enough, they don't matter, and no one really cares. They will often keep people at arm's length in an attempt at self-protection, and they'll struggle with trust issues. At the first hint of criticism, they shut down or blow up. A childhood and teen years that are deficient in genuine love, acceptance, and encouragement will affect their future relationships, marriage, leadership skills, and job opportunities.

Think about it – if God the Father took the time to break through the clouds of heaven to say these things to His Son, shouldn't we take the time to break through our schedule, our insecurities, and our pride, and do the same for our own sons and daughters?

Yes, the teenage room is often a messy room with cluttered shelves, piled-up clothes, and something nasty growing in the corner. But it is a crucial room in the home, and it needs special attention. For our homes to become more healthy and happy, we have to take the time to provide this essential information to our teenagers. We need to speak those words that will echo in their minds and hearts throughout their lives. Doing this will make the admittedly scary zip line ride across this adolescent canyon a more pleasurable experience not only for them, but also for the parents. Grab your teenager, take a deep breath, and zip away!

Small Group Questions:

1. How did your parents respond to you when you became a teenager? Would you describe their behavior as balanced? Over-reactionary? Uninvolved?

2. What did/do you fear about your child becoming a teenager?

3. How often do you tell your child that you love them? Is there any way they might believe your love for them is based upon some kind of performance on their part? Why is performance-based love and acceptance so harmful?

4. Make a list of what makes you proud of each of your children. Make a commitment to communicate this to your child today!

5. If God the Father communicated vital information to His Son, Jesus, why is it important for parents to express the same things to our children? What are the potential consequences if we withhold this information from our children?

"No amount of ability is of the slightest avail without honor."
Thomas Carlyle

Chapter Four
The Living Room: Honor

Every generation, as far back as anyone can remember, shares one common trait – the absolute conviction that the up-coming generation is the most disrespectful collection of ruffians ever to make their jeans-clad, short-skirted, belly-baring, pants-dragging way onto the planet. It's probably always been this way, but maybe I'm reaching the age where I just notice this like never before.

I recently saw a news story featuring a parking lot security video of an elderly man arriving at his car after he'd finished his grocery shopping. As soon as he unlocked his car, several suspicious-looking guys rushed over from the sidewalk where they'd been waiting for anyone who looked vulnerable enough to overpower. They jumped him, beat him up, and threw him to the ground. The young hoodlums then piled into his car and drove it away, leaving the man lying there on the pavement. The video also captured footage that was equally horrifying in its own way: Less than ten yards away, a group of people stood by, just watching the attack, and not one of them made a move to intervene. When the assault was complete they quickly went back to their conversation, casually chatting while the old man twisted on the ground in pain.

Two teenagers came into my friend's tuxedo shop one day in preparation for their upcoming prom. The boyfriend introduced himself and the young lady at his side: "This is my ho and I am her pimp." Nice way to refer to your girlfriend, man. Real nice. Very honoring!

Is it just me, or does it seem to you that increasingly younger children are using the foulest of language? Whether they are talking to their parents, teachers, or coaches, they say whatever they want without hesitation or regret. There is no filter between their brains and their mouths. They just say whatever is on their mind, and all too often there are no consequences for their rudeness.

We are surrounded by a culture of disrespect and dishonor. You find it on crowded buses where men are sitting comfortably in seats while women and the elderly are standing. It shows up in the marketplace where disinterested and downright rude customer service is now the norm, and in the common attitude among employees that their boss has no right to tell them what to do. It shows up on people wearing sexually graphic t-shirts without shame, and in rude drivers who give people the bird at the slightest offense.

Why is this? I have two theories. First, we have trained several generations to cherish the mentality that "The world revolves around me." They have been allowed - and even encouraged – to do what they want to do, say what they want to say, wear what they want to wear, and act however they want to act. God help the individual who dares to correct them, discipline them or hold them accountable for their words and actions!

Secondly, we are experiencing what I call a "Trickle-Down Morality." The pervasive lack of honor and respect for God in our culture is trickling down into relationships of every kind. Therefore, we see fewer and fewer people showing respect or honor toward authority of *any* kind. (Of course, this attitude suddenly changes when *they* are the ones in authority!) For nearly 40 years we have seen a growing lack of honor and respect for human life at the earliest stages of life, and now it is appearing in shifting attitudes toward the sick, the elderly, and the disabled. More and more groups of people are endangered as our culture becomes increasingly less willing to value life.

Teachers, coaches, employers, and society in general are at a loss to find a cure for this contagious disrespect. The Louisiana state legislature recently went so far as to pass a law requiring students to address teachers with at least an outward appearance of respect and honor by referring to them as "Ma'am" and "Sir." State Senator Don Cravins, one of the bill's co-sponsors, said in frustration, "The lack of respect in and out of school is a national problem, and no one has an answer."[3]

Should we throw our hands up in the air and sigh in resignation, "It is what it is and we can't do anything about it," or should we take a more targeted approach? I say it's the latter. Realistically, you may not be able to change the whole world, but you can influence your own home!

Here is a tried-and-true principle: A healthy home makes honor into an everyday habit. The opposite, however, is also true: An unhealthy home makes *dishonor* an everyday habit. Every home, whether intentionally or unintentionally, develops habits for those who live under its roof. Habits are actions that are repeated until they happen without much thought. They become instinctive and repetitive. We learn habits in our homes such as brushing our teeth, waking up at a certain time, falling into a routine for a typical Saturday, and doing our personal grooming. The things we see on a regular basis and do repeatedly are the behaviors that become habits.

One of the habits most families don't even realize they're developing is the way their family members talk to and treat each other in their home. These patterns subconsciously shape the way we talk to and treat other people outside of our home.

If we want to establish a healthy home that makes honor an everyday habit, we need to take a closer look at what *honor* actually means. The Hebrew word *kabad*, usually translated as "honor," also carries the meaning of "to be heavy; to be weighty." It carries with it the picture of an ancient caravan from the patriarchal times of Israel. When a caravan passed through the countryside, people stopped and took notice. Caravans traveled at a slow pace because they were weighted down with many goods, valuables, and every practical necessity for hundreds of nomads who would likely be on the move for weeks or months at a time. The ground-shaking rumble of the camels under their loads, the flashes of sun off of the women's coin-laden necklaces, the billowing robes of the men riding herd on the flocks, the calls of the birds that followed the bleating goats and sheep, the clouds of dust in their wake – if you were out working in your field when a caravan passed, you couldn't help but stand up and take notice. The sheer magnitude of the thing brought a sense of awe to all who were watching it pass by.

In our time, people's words, advice, and/or position can carry weight with us in the same way that the authority of one of these caravan leaders would have carried weight in ancient times. We honor who people are, what they say, and what they do. These things carry weight with us.

In the typical living room, you'll find objects of honor on display. In my home there are framed pictures of each of our girls from the current school year. We have a large puzzle framed and mounted on the wall. Every time we see the picture of the old-fashioned church in the meadow, it brings back memories of assembling it piece by piece as a family during one Christmas holiday. In our living room and throughout our home you will find my wife's treasured collection of Willow Tree angel figurines. Her collection of heirloom quilts and her grandmother's Bible also hold a special place of honor.

I remember a framed American flag that held a place of honor in the living room of my childhood home. It was given to our family when my grandfather, a World War I veteran, passed away. In my current community of Bremerton, Washington I have seen impressive shadow boxes mounted on living room walls in the homes of retired military personnel. These boxes house all the brightly colored awards and medals they accumulated over a lengthy Navy career, displaying with well-deserved pride the accomplishments of decades of service.

All of these are examples of honor. It isn't just a picture of some old folks on your living room wall – they are your grandparents. They carry weight because of their contribution to your DNA and your family heritage. It isn't just a framed photo of some random kid – it's your brother or your sister. They carry weight in your life because of years of shared laughter, memories, and life. It isn't just any wedding picture with funny-looking hair styles and an out-of-date tuxedo – it's your wedding portrait. It carries weight because it is a visual reminder of two people starting their new life together. And it isn't just a piece of colored cloth mounted on the wall – it's our national flag. It carries weight and value because it represents our freedom and the blood sacrificed that allows us to remain a free country.

God's Word tells us to make honor an everyday habit in our homes. It's a recurring theme throughout Scripture. The Ten Commandments are God's way of telling us how to live – they cover both vertical relationships (with God) and horizontal relationships (with other people). A closer look reveals that each commandment includes an aspect of honor.

1. Honor Me! Have no other gods.
2. Honor My worship! Don't worship idols.
3. Honor My name! Don't misuse it or treat it lightly.
4. Honor My day! Use the Sabbath for rest, not for work.
5. Honor your parents! Be respectful toward them.
6. Honor life! Don't murder.
7. Honor your marriage! Don't commit adultery.
8. Honor others' property! Don't steal.
9. Honor the truth! Don't lie.

10. Honor contentment! Don't covet things that
aren't yours.

God knows that when we build an everyday habit of honor in our life, all of our relationships are improved. Life is better all the way around. Without a habit of honor, we can quickly become self-centered. We begin poisoning, not blessing, every relationship around us.

Notice how this habit of honor in the home shows up in other Scriptures:

- *"Rise in the presence of the aged, show respect for the elderly and revere your God." (Leviticus 19:32)*
- *"Children, obey your parents...honor your father and mother." (Ephesians 6:1-2)*
- *"...the wife must respect her husband (Ephesians 5:33)*
- *"Husbands, in the same way be considerate as you live with your wives, and treat them with respect..." (I Peter 3:7)*

Outside of the family dynamic, I believe the best verse that covers all other forms of honor is found in I Peter 2:17. It says,

"Show proper respect to everyone: Love the brotherhood of believers, fear God, honor the king."

Are we to honor only the people we like and who are nice to us? Should we honor only those who come from similar backgrounds and who make us comfortable? No. We are to have a habit of honoring everyone, including those we worship with, work with, live with, and report to. Are we to honor only those whom we agree with politically? No. We are to even honor those government leaders with whom we strongly disagree. At the time of this biblical passage, Nero was the Emperor of Rome. He was a paranoid psychotic ruler who killed Christians for pleasure. Honor has no boundaries.

Making honor an everyday habit at home is hard work. Why? You live with your family in such close proximity that (if you're anything like my family!) you can aggravate each other now and then. Even though you love your family members, you hear them, see them, smell them, and sometimes grow weary of them. It requires a deliberate effort to develop an everyday habit of honor.

Making honor an everyday habit in the home means that honor is strategic, planned, and on our radar all the time. Honor does not happen in a home by accident. It is intentional.

Model It!

Children take their cues from Mom and Dad. They notice how their parents talk to and treat each other. They see the looks, the rolling of the eyes, and when we purposefully ignore each other, it doesn't escape their notice. They may be young, but our kids are not dumb. They also hear how we talk to them. Children seem to have an unerring instinct for the invisible line where we'll lose our patience, and they test us to see just how close they can come to it. They know if we have a habit of honoring them with our speech and our attitude even when we're completely exasperated with them.

Our children observe how we talk with our aged parents, and just as importantly, they hear what we say about them after we hang up the phone. Our kids see how we treat the teachers and coaches that we tell them to respect. Our children notice how we talk to strangers, and you'd better believe they're sitting in the back seat with their ears wide open to every word that flies out of our mouths when we get cut off in traffic. Whether we realize it or not, we are modeling honor all the time.

Our girls, like any kids their age, sometimes come home from school frustrated at a particular teacher. After they describe the situation, I've sometimes found myself becoming frustrated as well! One of my hot buttons is any teacher who believes it is a mark of toughness when no one in the class passes one of their tests. In my opinion, if everyone fails, the teacher has failed. They were either unclear or unprepared to adequately teach the subject to their students. They have failed to do their job.

In situations like this one, I have a choice as a parent. I could easily go off on the teacher in front of my kids. I could whine, complain, and gripe that I'm spending hard-earned money to send them to school, and that my girls deserve better. This may be true, but voicing this opinion to them is unwise.

I wish I had more time to coach my girls in sports, but since my schedule won't allow it, I have to submit to whatever coach my girls receive. There have been times when the coach was superb, and showing them honor was easy. There have been other times, though, when the coach was less than stellar. When a coach doesn't teach the fundamentals, plays favorites with certain players, or doesn't recognize the effort and skill of my girls, I struggle to keep my composure. My competitive nature tells me that I could do a much better job and that I should just step in and take over. I'm tempted to show the coach up, but I know this would be disrespectful, and I have to make a conscious choice not to engage in behavior that would dishonor them. I might truly wish my girls had better coaches, but it would be wrong of me to broadcast this.

In both situations I have a critical choice to make: Undermine and dishonor their teacher or coach, or model honor even when it's difficult. After venting my frustrations to my wife in private, I have chosen to honor these authority figures in front of my girls. If they see dishonor and disrespect coming from me, I've just given my girls an excuse to show disrespect to someone in authority in their life. This is not a path I want to send my girls down.

Their eyes are always watching. Their ears are always hearing. When they witness honor as an everyday habit from me, they will begin to develop this habit for themselves.

Expect It!

Honoring each other is a basic expectation in our home. It has been that way since we brought each of our girls home from the hospital. I remember taking Ashley out to McDonald's on a daddy-daughter date a few days before she became a big sister for the first time. In between bites of French fries I explained to her how our home was about to change. I told her that our love had the capacity to expand beyond just Ashley, and that we were going to love this next little one just as much as we loved her. I then laid out some clear expectations of how I wanted her to act as a big sister. I understood that there was only so much a four-year-old could comprehend and remember, but I wanted to lay the groundwork of what was coming, and what would be expected of her. The key would be repeating these expectations early and often.

Candy is the real reason why our girls love each other so much today. She was a mama on a mission! She was determined that our girls would develop great friendships with their sisters. We figured they had no choice in who they got as a sister, but they did have a choice about how they treated each other. Candy reinforced over and over, "You will be kind to each other!" "You do not talk that way to your sister!" "You will share that toy or that toy will be taken away, and *no one* will play with it!" When I asked them recently what they remembered Candy saying on this subject, they laughed and replied in unison: "Girls – kind talking!"

As the saying goes, "You inspect what you expect!" And Candy was inspecting *all* the time, like a military officer in charge of her troops. She monitored the tone, tenor, and volume of each girl toward the others. She even monitored their looks and the way they rolled their eyes. Constant reminders echoed from Mom: "You didn't say it nice. Try it again!" "I know you're tired. That's not an excuse to be mean to her!" She would even bust out the all-time classic, "If you can't say something nice, don't say anything at all!"

Because we wanted our girls to treat each other with respect and honor and eventually become close friends, this became the standard in our home. It wasn't enforced on an emotional whim or ignored when Candy became too tired to deal with it. Eventually she wore them down and won out over time. Now, if Candy hears a conversation in the other room taking a certain trajectory, all she has to say is, "Girls!" and we'll hear their voices calling back, "We know. I'm sorry, Holly, will you forgive me?"

Now, our girls are not perfect, and they still definitely have their moments. But for the most part, we've now reached the destination we charted years ago. They love each other. Their relationship carries weight with each other. They have developed the hard-earned habit of honoring each other.

We recently had a sleepover at our house. Since I don't want to scar anyone for life, that's the time I have to remind myself to make sure I wear a T-shirt and basketball shorts in the early morning instead of wandering around the house shirtless and wearing my boxer shorts. Anyway, on the second day I overheard a conversation between one of the girls and my youngest daughter. The conversation went something like this:

> "You actually *like* your sister?" she asked
> "Well, yeah!" Kailey replied.
> "You mean you don't fight?" her friend asked.
> "No. It's not something we do."
> "Man, I fight with my sisters all the time!"

What was normal for her friend was abnormal to my daughter. Is this because my girls are so special, better or unique? No. They were born sinners just like everybody else. They just happened to be born into a home where showing dishonor was not an option.

Candy and I are now enjoying the fruit of many years of hard work toward an everyday habit of honor with our girls.

They actually love being together now. They have special sister sleepovers, sister movie nights, and take over the kitchen for the evening to make brownies. They made so many hilarious "Bandara Sisters" music videos together that they blew through the entire memory capacity on our family computer. Ashley is heading off to college in a few months, and I've already come across notes to Ashley from her sisters telling her how much they will miss her, how much they love her, and how thankful they are for her. Priceless!

Teach It!

If making honor an everyday habit in our homes is a priority, we must take advantage of the teachable moments that are all around us. We must learn to see those opportunities when they appear. We need to stop, get our children's attention, and point out the lessons we want them to learn:

- "Did you see that boy on the playground and how he was talking to his mommy? We don't talk that way. That was disrespectful."
- "Did you hear how that girl spoke to her father on TV? That was not respectful or appropriate."
- "I don't like how people are talking to each other and treating each other on this show. Hand me the remote, I'm changing the channel."

When we stop, get their attention, and point out disrespectful behavior, we are giving our kids memorable visual examples of what they should or should not do. We are providing them with real-life illustrations that will make lasting impressions in their young minds, reinforcing what we're trying to teach them at home. If developing an everyday habit of honor is not on your radar, you will miss the tremendous teachable moments that are at your disposal.

Correct It!

If dishonor and disrespect are not corrected, they will become the established habit, as surely as any other behavior that's repeated over time. I'll talk more in detail about discipline in another chapter, but I must at least mention it here. When dishonor goes unchecked, you are giving it oxygen and credibility.

When a teacher allows disrespect in their classroom and nothing happens, it's open season from that point on. When a coach is treated disrespectfully by a player and it isn't dealt with, the coach's authority and credibility are undermined.

In addition to the "weight" we want our girls to give to each other as sisters, we teach and correct them when it comes to honoring us as their parents. The role parents play in the life of their children is enormous, and it is worthy of being treated with respect. The Bible's command for children to honor their parents is followed with a special additional blessing:

> *"Honor your father and mother – which is the first commandment with a promise – that it may go well with you and that you may enjoy long life on the earth." (Ephesians 6:2-3)*

First, I tell my children that life will go well with them when they honor their parents. They will receive more freedom and privileges when they honor us. Dishonor brings less freedom and fewer privileges. It's that simple. Second, I simplify the promise to, "You will enjoy life" if you honor your parents. The opposite is true as well: "You will not enjoy life if you are disrespectful!" Again, it's not that complicated to me. Life is better for them – and for their parents! – when honor is an everyday habit. Life experience tells us that disrespectful, undisciplined children sometimes live shorter lives due to the results of their poor choices, and our prisons are full of those who are paying the price for lives lived with a lack of discipline and respect for authority.

In my home, my shortest fuse is lit when Candy is not treated with honor and respect. For all of her cooking, cleaning, helping with homework and projects, taxi driving, picture-taking, more cleaning, more cooking, and more errands – not to mention a week in labor and childbirth – she has earned a lifetime of honor from her children!

I normally do not raise my voice in my house, but there are two exceptions to this rule. When the 49ers score a touchdown or when I see any one of my girls disrespecting their mother, I tend to rattle the rafters. My girls hear me loud and clear when I say, "You *will not* talk to your mother this way!" Because I don't normally lose my cool, when I do, it has the proper effect. One night when one of my very hormonal adolescents flippantly mouthed off to her mother, I dropped a new line that took her by surprise: "You will not treat *my wife* this way!" She knew I meant it.

If we ignore or refuse to correct disrespect, we will go backward in making honor an everyday habit in our home. We lose. They lose.

Praise It!

Praise goes a long way toward encouraging any habit. Although we respond to correction, praise takes us farther and faster down the path. When we are praised for correct behavior it sends a positive signal to our brain that says, "Do that again!" That's why dog trainers hand out more dog treats than harsh words to get their animals to respond in the way they want them to.

I'm not saying our children are animals. Well, OK, sometimes their eating habits might make us second-guess that assessment. But the truth of the matter is that all of us respond to praise. It goes a long way when we praise our kids for demonstrating honor:

- "Thank you for saying what you said the way you did. Even though you were upset, you communicated with respect."

- "I watched how you handled what your coach said to you. It must have been hard to hear, but you responded really well. Great job!"
- "I know Nana is repeating herself a lot lately. That's what happens when you're in your 90's. That was respectful, the way you patiently listened to the same story again."
- "I see the way you treat others who are younger than you. Keep it up. They look up to you."

Again, we must take these teachable moments with our kids and use them to our advantage at every opportunity.

The Result

Making honor an everyday habit at home will transfer to every area of our children's lives. It will travel to school with them. It will go with them into the workplace. It will journey into every relationship they have. They will carry it with them into their community. It will eventually find its way into the next generation when they begin building their own happy and healthy homes.

So what's the condition of your living room? I'm not referring to your color schemes and furniture layout. I'm talking about honor in your home. Some of you simply need to be encouraged to keep up the good work and continue making strides to instill a healthy DNA of honor in your home. You may be tired and worn out by addressing it all the time. Trust me, in time it *will* be worth it.

Others of you might have some work to do. Your home may have an unhealthy habit of dishonor. First, start with yourself. Make an honest evaluation of how you honor or dishonor your parents, your boss, your spouse, and your children. Resist the urge to give a defensive, "Yeah, but" for your dishonoring behavior. Second, you may need to sit your family down and apologize for allowing disrespect to grow as much as it has in your home. Be humble enough to say, "I haven't done a good job and I've failed in this area. But with God's help, starting with me, we will make honor a habit in this home." Changing a habit of dishonor to a habit of honor will take time. One announcement at a family meeting will not be enough. Third, be firm and be consistent. Over time the tide will change in a positive direction.

A home cannot be healthy and happy without honor becoming an everyday habit. Begin today by cleaning up your living room!

Small Group Questions:

1. Without a habit of honor, people become self-centered. How does this poison the relationships surrounding the self-centered individual?

2. Why is honor becoming a rare commodity these days? What does it look like when a home does not exhibit honor?

3. What cues, good or bad, have your children taken from you in regards to honoring other people – drivers, relatives, authority figures, etc.?

4. How do you show honor and respect to your children? How do you show honor and respect to your spouse or ex-spouse?

5. If you have more than one child, what are your goals for them as siblings? What kind of behavior do you want and expect from them in relationship to each other? Why do many siblings treat each other with such dishonor and disrespect?

"I am definitely going to take a course on time management...just as soon as I can work it into my schedule."
Louis E. Boone

Chapter Five
The Map Room: Calendar Essentials

Time seemed to move slowly when I was younger. Summer break seemed to last forever. Now, it feels like time is moving much faster the older I get. I think this summer lasted about two weeks. My high-energy personality means I don't mind a fast pace, but if I'm not careful I can easily become oblivious to the fact that life is passing by, and quickly! My wife, on the other hand, is the one in our family who occasionally shouts "STOP!" and forces our family to come to a grinding halt. She marches us all into what I like to call the Map Room, and she starts asking the hard questions about exactly what we're doing and why. I'm thankful that at least one of us has this ability, because she helps our home maintain much-needed health and sanity.

You may be saying to yourself, "Map Room? We don't have one of those in our house." Let me explain. The Map Room is a room on the ground floor of the White House. It received its name during World War II when President Franklin Roosevelt used it as a situation room to track the war's progress. Officers assigned to the Map Room maintained up-to-the-minute maps, charts and files concerning all the active battles in Europe and in the Pacific. President Roosevelt wanted to have an accurate accounting of all the land and naval forces of the United States, its allies, and their enemies, and he chose this room as the centralized location to gather all of this information into one place.

We do have a Map Room in our homes, and it is the family calendar. Whether real or imaginary, our calendar indicates the up-to-the-minute movement of our family. Many family calendars are busy and full of activities – practices and games to attend, trips to take, project and assignment due dates, along with the inevitable appointments for the dentist, the doctor, the orthodontist, the butcher, the baker, and the candlestick maker. If we wonder why we are more stressed than ever before, a good look at our calendars will quickly answer that question!

A satellite view from outer space would make most families look like an ant farm – full of hustle and bustle, never slowing down, scrambling around to the point of exhaustion, and bumping into each other constantly. Most families today are hurried, hassled, stressed and strained. They regularly find themselves coming and going, rushing out of the home in the morning and rushing home later in the day, only to rush out again at night.

In many ways, our families are in a battle – a battle of priorities. If we don't take the time to account for all the movement of our family now and then, we can easily become overwhelmed with all that we have to do. From painfully hard-earned experience, I know my primary symptom when my activity levels edge up into the red zone: I start forgetting things. I'm supposed to be driving across town for soccer practice but my car is chugging happily along to work, with me at the wheel in a fog, in the opposite direction from the soccer field. I'll call someone on the phone, and while it is ringing my mind wanders off to all the other things on my "to do" list. Then when they answer the phone, I've already forgotten who I've called. They say, "Hello?" and I have to sheepishly ask, "Uh, who am I talking to?"

I believe that many homes are unhealthy and unhappy because instead of being in control of their calendars, their calendars are controlling them. A family can quickly become disjointed and disconnected when their long lists of activities are allowed to dictate their schedules. All too easily, they can discover that they have spent months or years living together without really knowing each other.

Running on Empty

King Solomon's life helps us gain a healthy perspective on time management. His wisdom and hard-won experience are valuable resources when we're making a deliberate effort to spend our time and energy on what is truly important. Solomon wrote the book of Ecclesiastes after many years of pouring vast amounts of time and money into a whirlwind of pursuits. He explains his initial motivation for these projects:

> "I wanted to see what was worthwhile for men to do under heaven during the few days of their lives." (Ecclesiastes 2:3)

Then he continues in verses 4-9 with a detailed list of the activities that filled his time. You think you've got a crazy calendar? Check out this guy's daily planner: He built houses, planted vineyards, laid out gardens, parks and orchards (notice how all of these are plural, not singular!), built reservoirs to keep them green and flourishing, bought slaves to work in his houses and fields, amassed great herds and flocks of animals, made hundreds of marriage alliances for political and personal reasons, and acquired singers and treasures for his own enjoyment. His projects were creative, industrious, and financially profitable. Aside from the harem and the slaves, this list is one that would be a noble and attention-getting accomplishment even in today's world of great businessmen and overachievers.

In verse 10 he continues:

> "I denied myself nothing my eyes desired; I refused my heart no pleasure. My heart took delight in all of my work, and this was the reward for all of my labor. Yet when I surveyed all that my hands had done and what I toiled to

achieve, everything was meaningless, a chasing after the wind; nothing was gained under the sun." (Ecclesiastes 2:10-11)

Although Solomon took delight in all of the creativity and industry that filled up his calendar, something was missing. Even after all of his effort, he was still empty. He summed up his years of work as simply "chasing the wind," with nothing of true and lasting value to show for it!

This phrase, "a chasing after the wind", shows up nine different times in this autobiography. Solomon chased after knowledge and wisdom – empty. He ran after pleasure – empty. He pursued work, relationships, and riches – empty again. The word "chasing" in the original Hebrew language means *"striving; longing."* This implies an intense effort and a great exertion of energy. I think the Webster's Online Dictionary's definition of "chase" accurately describes Solomon's calendar: *"an earnest or frenzied seeking after something."* In his final evaluation Solomon says, "It wasn't worth it!"

The Essential Over the Non-Essential

If Solomon were here today I believe he would say to us, "I chased non-essentials, and I ended up wasting my energy, effort, money, and time. If I could do it all over again, I would chase the essential instead of the non-essential. I would say 'no' to the immediate in order to say 'yes' to the important!"

If we are honest with ourselves, many of our family calendars show clear indications that we are "chasing after the wind." This certainly doesn't mean that everything we are doing needs to be discarded, but rather that the non-essentials are crowding out the essentials. The immediate is overriding the important.

When I was a junior at Liberty University we were challenged to sit down and come up with a priority list so we could divert our time, energy and attention to what was essential.

Since I've never liked following the crowd, I went ahead and made up my list ... but with an attitude.

I pulled out a blank piece of paper and typed in a large font at the top of the page, "MY PRIORITY LIST." I then typed the numbers 1 through 10 down the left side of the page. But I purposefully left each item blank. Nothing. No details. Now, when someone asked me if I had a priority list, I could respond with all confidence and truthfulness that I indeed had a priority list!

One afternoon a guy in my dorm asked me if I wanted to do something that I didn't really want to do at all. I replied, "Let me first take a look at my Priority List." I went over to my posted list and proclaimed, "Sorry, I can't. It's not on my Priority List." He said, "I don't see anything!" "Believe me," I said, "It's not on the list!" A few days later another guy knocked on my door and asked, "Hey, do you want to go golfing with us?" I calmly answered, "Let me first take a look at my Priority List." I walked over, looked over my list and exclaimed, "Yep! There it is! Number 3 on the list! Let me grab my clubs!"

Besides confirming that I was young, immature, and occasionally arrogant in college, this example demonstrates another common fault: We do the things we want to do. If we aren't careful, this can prove to be unhealthy, unwise, and a colossal waste of time.

When it comes to our family, we don't have time to waste! Before we know it, our children will be grown up, out of the house, and on their own. We don't have the capability to rewind the time and try it again. More importantly, if we spend our time on the non-essentials in life we are providing a great disservice to our kids. They will most likely enter their adult years with a warped view of what is really important in life. They will then move forward with a twisted sense of priorities and a value system that you may not approve of – even though, in truth, it was based on the value system they learned from you. As for me, I don't want to look back and agonize like Solomon, saying, "It was a chasing after the wind! Our calendar was full of things that didn't really matter!"

Healthy Essentials
God

A healthy home has God at the top of the priority list. As an individual, having God as my top priority involves more than what I put on my calendar. It involves my heart, my attitude, and having a personal and active prayer life. It also shows up in how I respond to people in my life. I believe that having God as my top priority also includes consistent and regular church attendance. As a family unit, making God our top priority shows up in a variety of ways: thanking God for His blessings, praying together as a family, and serving our family members with genuine love.

Having God as a top priority in our family will also be evident on our family calendar. Our family is involved in an unseen war against a real enemy. His name is Satan. One of his strategies is to distract families to move in so many directions that God is shifted out of the top position on our priority list. With this in mind, let me ask several tough questions: How many weekends a month does your family attend church? What takes priority on your weekends?

The Apostle Paul gives us helpful instruction when it comes to our priorities in our lives and homes.

> *"He (Jesus) is before all things, and in him all things hold together. And he is the head... so that in everything He might have the supremacy." (Colossians 1:17-18)*

The word *supremacy* is another way of describing something or someone who is in the #1 position. When God is not ranked #1 in a family, everything begins to unravel and become unbalanced. The good becomes the enemy of the great, and the blessing of God is diminished. However, when a family has God

74

firmly and consistently entrenched as the top essential in their home, the hand of blessing from God is upon this family. This time-tested principle is true: God honors those who honor Him.

Does this mean that a God-honoring home is immune to trials and difficulties? Absolutely not. Every home is affected, and none are exempt from the repercussions of living in this sin-fallen world. But I have seen over and over that the home that has habitually placed God in His rightful position is usually the home that is better able to endure the difficult days when trials and problems do come. This is the home that is actually brought closer together and held together by God, instead of being torn apart when the storms of life hit.

While I was a high school pastor in southern California we were reacquainted with some distant family relatives. The parents had grown up in church and were spiritually grounded at an early age. But over the years, the temptations of non-essentials continued to take more and more ground in their hearts, and these changed values eventually showed up on their family calendar. For them, the non-essentials were fun toys like dirt bikes, quads, boats, and an RV. What started as a good thing (spending time together as a family) eventually began to take a negative toll. A weekend at the river, every so often, became a regular habit for them and their three boys.

Over time the parents discovered that their two oldest sons, now in their early twenties, had very little interest in church, and their youngest son didn't have a personal relationship with God at all. This greatly concerned them, so they asked me for help in getting their youngest son Mike (not his real name) involved in our high school group because, as they very accurately put it, "He needs God."

I was able to spend some good time with Mike and develop a relationship with him. He and his parents came back to church and Mike slowly got involved with our group. After several months of regular attendance, I asked him to come to our Winter

Camp up in the mountains of Big Bear, California. He was a little nervous at first, but once I mentioned snowboarding he was all in. He had a great camp experience and I could see the walls coming down between him and our group. He participated in a small group at camp, and I could tell he was glad he'd decided to come.

A few weeks after Winter Camp I gave a talk in our Sunday morning high school gathering that had a clear salvation message. I still remember the excitement I felt when I gave the call for students to make a decision to accept Christ as their Savior, and I looked up into the crowd and saw him raising his hand. I then led the students who wanted to receive Christ in a prayer of salvation.

As soon as the service ended I bolted up the amphitheater steps to talk with Mike. I wanted to know if he clearly understood the gospel and what he had just prayed. He did! He was so excited, and he was eager to tell his parents. I walked with him from the youth room, and we found them waiting for him in our crowded lobby. When Mike shared with his parents the eternal decision he had just made, his father broke out with a huge smile while his mom began to tear up. What an answer to prayer!

The next weekend I noticed that Mike wasn't there. The following weekend he missed church again. I called and left a message for him, but he didn't call back. A couple of weeks later he showed up again, but shortly thereafter he stopped coming all together. Nothing negative had happened. There was no antagonism toward God, me, or our high school group. Eventually, I found out that the river had drawn Mike away from the good habits he had started – the cool toys and trips to the river replaced his spiritual thirst for God.

Today, years later, all three sons are grown and out of the house. The last I heard, the parents are once again concerned about the spiritual well-being of their boys, since none of the three have any real interest in God or the church. My heart breaks to know of nice and genuinely well-meaning parents who nonetheless taught their sons to worship at the altar of non-essentials.

Let me be clear about two things: First, attending church every week is not the *only* way to determine one's true priorities with God. There are plenty of people whose body is at church but their heart is cold toward God. Secondly, making sure your children are at church on a regular basis is not a guarantee that they will choose to make God a top priority in their life. But I can say, based upon twenty-five years of pastoral experience, that families who choose to attend church on a consistent basis tend to win in the battle of priorities more than those who do not.

There is nothing wrong with an occasional weekend filled with fun and toys. The issue is what we are *chasing* after. Every toy will eventually break and be replaced with new ones, and you can never regain time that is wasted in "chasing after the wind." Worse yet, developing the habit of chasing after non-essentials can have eternal consequences for future generations.

Our lives are surrounded by many beneficial and valuable things like education, sports, friends, hobbies, and entertainment choices. These can be very good things that add flavor to life. However, they cannot be *more* important than the most important essential in life: God! Satan knows this and has schemed against us by using the non-essentials of life to crowd out the most essential.

Family
After God, a healthy and happy home places the family in the #2 position of healthy essentials, making the marriage, sibling relationships, and extended family part of that high priority. This is a home where high fives and hugs are commonplace. It is a home where birthdays are celebrated, games are attended, pictures are taken and plenty of memories are made.

In the movie *Leap Year*, the question is asked, "If there was a fire in the house and you only had 60 seconds, what would you take with you?" How would you answer that question? I would choose our family photo albums and our family DVDs. I can buy new furniture, computers, and appliances, but our albums and home movies are priceless because they contain irreplaceable memories of our family – the five of us on vacation, attending plays and games, being silly, and going through all the precious stages of life we've shared together.

God designed the family as the ultimate small group. It is intended to be a safe place where life is lived together. So our family has chosen to attend each other's events, games, and shows. Whether it was sitting together in a dark theater watching Ashley in her drama queen glory or huddling under umbrellas at a rain-drenched soccer game, we were there, all of us, because our family is #2 on our priority list. We strategically position our "troops" in our Map Room so that we can be there to support and encourage each other.

This is easier said than done. In 1998, my calendar was out of balance and out of control. While God was still in His rightful top position, my family was not in second position. I would publicly say that they were, and in my own mind this was true, but the practical truth was that my ministry was a higher priority than my family. Serving Jesus had shifted away from reaching teenagers for God to an addiction to activity. There were summer camps, winter camps, mission trips, weekly teaching, retreats, staff recruiting, writing midweek curriculum, games to attend, video footage to take, ministry basketball leagues to run, counseling to do, and student ministry teams to train. They were all good things. Students were coming to Christ and our ministry was growing in leaps and bounds. But while the ministry was healthy, my home was not.

I remember when Ashley, who was about 4 or 5 years old at the time, tried to get my attention at home – "Daddy," she said. "Daddy!" Over and over she called out to me, but my mind was so preoccupied with other things that I didn't recognize what she was doing. She then changed tactics and said, "Pastor Barry!" I am ashamed to say that I immediately turned my head and noticed her. I still can't believe my own warped thinking one rainy Friday night when I somehow justified leaving a sick wife at home with two young girls so that I could meet some students at a local football game. What an idiot!

One Sunday night after church, Candy quietly confronted me in the kitchen. All she said was, "Honey, I am excited to see what God is doing in the youth group, but we are getting lefto-vers." Usually I can come back with a quick comment or de-fense, but I had no answer this time. Her assessment was dead on and I had no comeback. Instead, I felt repressed emotion coming to the surface, and I began to tear up. All I could say was, "What do I stop?" She answered very tenderly, "I don't know, but something has to change."

In short order, major changes were made. I canceled a num-ber of activities completely and began to delegate ministry to my staff like never before. After making these changes behind the scenes, I found myself standing before a large group of par-ents who were eagerly waiting to hear about the next year's ministry plan. I confessed my unbalance and expressed that I wasn't pleased with the kind of husband and father I was be-coming. I then explained the necessary cutbacks and changes. I closed by saying, "The bottom line is this: My children are more important to me than yours." God surprised me. The parents overwhelmingly supported me and encouraged me for making these changes. On top of it all, the ministry grew more that year than ever. I am thankful that I learned this valuable lesson in time for me to recover health and balance for myself and my family.

Work

We enjoy having food to eat in our home. In fact, we try to make eating an everyday habit. Therefore, work is an essential because it's necessary to pay the bills, put food in our mouths, and clothes on our back. We can be confident that work itself is not part of the curse, since it was part of Adam's job description in the Garden of Eden. The curse of sin just made work harder. Work, however hard, can bring glory to God when we put it in its proper place and work as unto the Lord. In fact, it can be a gift from God. As Solomon states,

> "Moreover, when God gives any man wealth and posses-
> sions, and enables him to enjoy them, to accept his lot and
> be **happy in his work** – this is a gift from God." (Ecclesi-
> astes 5:19, emphasis added)

Work can quickly throw our priorities out of balance because we gain so much of our sense of significance from what we do. I know I do. If we are not careful, work can climb the essential chart and take over second position, or even bump God out of first place in our lives. When this happens, we are paying a high price for temporary dividends. A new car and a nice home are great things, but not at the expense of shifting the family down to a lower priority. Shortchanging our children in their forma-tive years will carry a steep price tag down the road.

I remember a time when my father was struggling to make ends meet. He was frustrated with too much month at the end of each paycheck. His perspective completely changed the day he stopped by the hospital to visit his friend, who was dying of throat cancer. Here lay a multimillionaire in the hospital whose sons refused to visit because he had no relationship with them. This man was actually jealous of my father and our family, even though we had so much less in terms of material things! He had spent all of his time, effort, and energy "chasing the wind" to build a career and to make money, but at the terrible cost of los-ing his family. His deathbed revealed that there really is no competition between the immediate and the important.

Little did my father realize that in a few short years he would find himself on his own deathbed. The significant and wonderful difference was that his family gathered by his side to honor his life and say goodbye. Although my father didn't leave us any financial wealth to speak of, he left a family who knew that we were always a higher priority than any job he held.

I agree with marriage and family expert Mark Gungor's assessment that men, generally speaking, compartmentalize life into different boxes. They have a box for their job, a box for their family, a box for their hobbies, etc. When this is true, they rearrange their boxes when attempting to prioritize, being careful that the boxes stay separate.[4] This is different for many women because everything in life seems to touch everything else. That's why I believe it can be more challenging for women than for men to prioritize their "work", because their work encompasses every aspect of their lives. Whether they have a career outside the home or they are stay-at-home mothers, their work is never done.

A 2007 survey done by Salary.com estimated that the typical mother puts in a 92-hour workweek *at home* doing an estimated 10 different jobs such as: Cook, Psychologist, Housekeeper, Laundry Machine Operator, Van Driver, CEO, Janitor, Day Care Center Teacher, Facilities Manager, and Computer Operator. This survey revealed that if they were compensated for their hours at these jobs at the going market rates, moms would make a salary of nearly $140,000 a year![5]

Beyond the physical drain a mom's life entails, she has the emotional drain of caring for sick kids, hearing the word "mommy" 250 times a day, fighting off the mental game of comparison with those apparent "super moms", and trying to stay awake for her husband at the end of the day when she is completely out of energy. Even if she is fortunate to have a husband who helps with the children, the meals, or housework, there are never enough days in the week to fully meet all the needs of her husband, her children, and her responsibilities outside the home. That's why it's critically important that essentials take priority on the family calendar before her family has to visit her in the padded room.

Here are several suggestions that were given to me by other mothers. It is not an exhaustive list, but I hope they will be of help and encouragement – especially to those moms with several ankle biters still at home.

- It's okay to ask for help. Ask your husband to take the kids for a walk around the block when he gets home from work – they could probably all use the fresh air, and it will give you a moment alone, or some one-on-one time with a child who needs your attention. Call a friend with young children to see if you can swap a few hours of childcare. If you don't have close friends and family nearby, your church might have more help available than you realize – there may be an older lady who would be delighted to keep an eye on your wakeful infant so you could grab a quick nap, and the youth pastor may have recommendations for mature, reliable students who could give you a hand for a few hours after school now and then. If a little help makes you a better mother, GO FOR IT!

- Outside of your main priorities, be picky about what you say "yes" to. Ask yourself: Do we really need to do this? Can this wait until later? I volunteered at school last month – can someone else volunteer this time? Do I really have the time and energy to make this commitment?

- Schedule an occasional time or day for yourself. Put it on the calendar if necessary, and don't feel guilty about it! My wife would do this now and then in order to keep her sanity. She loved being our girls' mother, but she occasionally needed to escape to a place where nobody was going to call her "Mommy." Sometimes she would be gone for several hours at a time, or take an entire Saturday for herself. It was worth its weight in gold for her as a wise and beneficial investment in her well-being.

- Sitting down to read the Bible or spending alone time with God is often difficult when your children are young. My friend, Shannon Bieger, recently shared with me that she listens to podcasts or worship music while she vacuums or cleans the house. She is like most mothers – masters at multi-tasking!

- Ask God for discernment between the immediate and the important. My friend and mother of three young children, Lindsay Manchester, recently shared with me her choice in the battle between her tasks as a mom and playing with her kids. She is beginning to choose more playtimes over the immediate task at hand. The kitchen will eventually get clean, but the ten minutes on the floor with her children is of greater value to her now.

Whether you are a man or a woman or a single parent or married couple, the battle to prioritize our work is a very difficult thing to do. Because work is so necessary for the survival of our family, it can easily creep its way up to a higher priority level than it should. Let me encourage you to ask God for wisdom in determining what is essential, and for the strength to accomplish what needs to get done each day.

Everything Else
After God, family, and work comes everything else. Whether it is education, sports, hobbies, friends, or entertainment, as long as they remain in the fourth position of priorities, you will simply add flavor to a healthy and happy home. When we pursue the essentials, we usually end up enjoying the non-essentials even more!

To illustrate this, take a large jar and fill it about three-quarters of the way with sand. The sand represents the non-essential things in life. Then find three large rocks about the size of your fists. These rocks represent life's essentials – your top priorities of God, family, and work. After the sand is in the jar, begin placing the large rocks inside. You will find that they won't all fit inside the jar. Now, do this again but in a different order. First, place the large rocks inside the jar. Then pour the sand in. You will discover that all of the sand will find its way inside the jar around the rocks.

The key is to begin *first* with the essentials in life, and all the non-essentials will fit around your life and family.

Whether you are President Roosevelt in the White House, King Solomon on the throne, my dad at the bedside of a broken millionaire, or a multi-tasking mom – take the time to map out the movement of your family. Map out the most strategic use of the time, energy, and money for your family. Invest time and energy into your family priority list, not only for your own health and sanity during the busy years when your family is all under one roof, but also as a powerful lifelong example to your children as they enter their own battles with priorities.

Small Group Questions:

1. Describe your family calendar. Is it hurried, hassled, stressed, and strained? If so, why?

2. Write down an accurate and current list of priorities of your family. What is your highest priority? Why? What needs to drop lower down the list, or off the list completely?

3. What non-essentials are you and your family chasing? If you need to say "no" to the immediate so you can say

"yes" to the important, what changes do you need to make to your priorities?

4. If there was a fire in your house and you had only 60 seconds, what would you take with you? Why?

5. We cannot reclaim time once it has passed. What do you need to rearrange in your schedule in order to create more memories for your family?

6. Schedule a time to do the rock and sand project with your family. Talk about this illustration with your children.

*"We should not be ashamed to talk about what God
wasn't too ashamed to create."*
Howard Hendricks

Chapter Six
The Master Suite: Fox Hunting!

A healthy and happy home must have a healthy and happy master bedroom. Some may call it the Master Suite. I call it the Master "Sweet" – as in *delicious!*

I do not believe that you can have true health and happiness in your home unless they flow from the cistern of the husband-and-wife relationship. I understand that there are single parent households that are healthy and happy, but experience indicates that this is the exception rather than the rule.

Despite our culture's desperate attempts to convince us otherwise, what's good for our children is for them to come home at night to a home with both a father and a mother. As a youth pastor, I told my students many times that, given our culture, if their parents still lived together and even *liked* each other, they were lucky! Let me state the obvious – the best-case scenario is for children to come home to a father and a mother who are still *in love* with each other. Imagine that! Sadly, this is rare these days.

So far we have inspected the kitchen, the kids' room, the teenagers' room, the living room, and the map room in our imaginary model home. I would be amiss to skip the master bedroom, since it is usually the largest bedroom in the house.

Sometimes I've referred to our bedroom as *"The Love Shack."* I'm pretty sure it embarrasses my wife every time I use this term, but since it also makes her laugh every time, and laughter always contains an element of truth, I continue to use it. Plus, she hasn't told me to stop – and the extra bonus that it also embarrasses my daughters makes me want to use it all the more!

The "S" Word

For many years, the "S" word was rarely mentioned in church. If you don't know what word I am referring to, let me help you out: It begins with "s" and ends with "x." That's right, SEX! If sex was ever mentioned in church, it was usually cast in a negative light. This unfortunately led several generations to believe that the church (and God) viewed sex to be wrong or dirty. What a foolish mistake! Many church leaders were duped by Satan into avoiding teaching this all-important subject in a biblical way. This lack of good teaching resulted in the church waving the white flag of surrender regarding this beautiful gift that God created for married couples.

This in turn allowed our culture to define the meaning and value of sex. Because the devil has no ability to create anything new, all he can do is twist and distort God's created masterpieces. It probably won't surprise anybody that Satan once again turned something beautiful into something debased and defiled.

God is crystal clear in his Word when He says,

> *"Marriage is to be held in honor among all, and the marriage bed is to be undefiled..."* (Hebrews 13:4, NASB)

God's design for marriage and sex within marriage is honorable and undefiled. The Greek word for undefiled is *amiantos*, which means "free from being deformed or debased." Just because our culture has deformed and debased sex with pornography, casual sex, "friends with benefits", sexting and various forms of immorality, this doesn't mean that God's view of sex, which He created for married couples, has changed in the slightest! The church has avoided speaking out on this subject for too long, and this silence has brought about devastating results. As Howard Hendricks, the beloved professor at Dallas Seminary, once said, "We should not be ashamed to discuss what God wasn't too ashamed to create." It's time to take back the precious ground we have surrendered!

Soon after becoming a senior pastor I did something completely unexpected for our conservative church: I taught a whole series on sex. When people entered the worship center at the start of the series, they were expecting the usual décor, the cross, and the podium. Instead, they found themselves face to face with a complete bedroom set right on the stage, surrounded with lit candles! After all the years I spent telling teenagers to say "no" to premarital sex, I was excited to teach that the Bible says a hearty "yes" to passionate, fulfilling, and satisfying sex for married couples.

Many people fail to remember that the Bible contains an entire book that talks about sex. The book is called Song of Songs, which is sometimes referred to as the Song of Solomon. In the first two chapters we witness the attraction, the flirtation, the pursuit, and finally the engagement of this beautiful couple. Chapter three is devoted to the wedding ceremony. And then, whoa! Hold on! Check out chapter four! While the wedding party is still celebrating outside, this chapter explicitly – and appropriately – takes us right into the bridal chamber.

Before I preached on this chapter, I felt like I should double check to make sure the church sprinkler system worked! I enjoyed the nervous laughter and tension in our worship center as we worked through this erotic chapter. Some of you have never read chapter four of the Song of Solomon, and you're tempted right now to bust out your Bible! When you do, you will find the new groom beginning with his bride's eyes and hair, and then complimenting her beauty as it is revealed while he undresses her.

At first glance, many readers won't understand the metaphors the writer is using, so if you think this language doesn't sound romantic in the least, you're not the only one. If a husband today lovingly whispered in his wife's ear, "Honey, your teeth are like a flock of sheep", all chances of any romantic action would be out the window! Understanding the meanings of the word pictures helps us understand that some serious verbal foreplay is going on. Trust me, this dude knew how to romance the girl! If not, the chapter wouldn't conclude with one of the most erotic verses in the Bible, with the bride calling out:

> *"Awake, north wind! Blow on my garden, that its fragrance may spread abroad. Let my lover come into his garden and taste its choice fruits." (Song of Songs 4:16)*

In this book a woman's sexuality is referred to as a "garden." The bride is saying in this verse, "Come into your garden, big boy – it's all-you-can-eat!" Not too surprisingly, he does so without hesitation!

If you think chapter four is hot, you need to check out chapter seven! While chapter four makes poetic hints and allusions to what is happening on their wedding night, chapter seven isn't so subtle. In fact, it invites its readers to watch the two lovers engage in the art of making love.

I'll let you study this chapter for yourself, but I will highlight that before the husband "climbs the palm tree and takes hold of the fruit", he showers her with praise, appreciation, respect, and admiration. This kind of verbal foreplay should not be limited to the master bedroom, expressed only in order to satisfy hormonally-driven physical desires. A healthy marriage with a healthy sex life is one that is manifested inside *and* outside the bedroom. You must have both.

My wife and I are not afraid to model for our children that we are still very much in love and attracted to each other. We don't hesitate to talk appropriately about sex and God's design for this wonderful gift. In addition to conversations about what is appropriate or inappropriate on television, Candy and I model for our girls what it looks like for a husband to continue in his pursuit of his wife, and how a wife responds to his flirtation.

We have also taken the time to share with each of our girls that the marriage bed is honorable and should not be not defiled. When we felt that our girls were old enough to be ready for this conversation, Candy has taken each of the girls separately on a special retreat where they walked through *Passport2Purity*, a resource for parents and kids published by FamilyLife. Each girl received one-on-one time with her mother to privately discuss their bodies, boys, sexuality, and the temptations they could expect in the years to come. This retreat included a stay at a nice hotel, their workbook and conversation sessions, shopping and a fun activity unique to each girl. Then, on their trip home, I'd meet up with them at a special restaurant to celebrate this milestone in our daughter's life. I would then have the chance to speak to my daughter from a man's perspective about this crucial subject. When our youngest daughter came home from her special retreat, the other two daughters were excited and relieved. One of them exclaimed, "Finally! Now we can talk about things without using code words anymore!" I also liked not having to explain anymore why our bedroom door was locked!

As parents, it was fun to watch each of them pass a milestone in their life after coming home from their retreat. We didn't want them to receive this sensitive and precious information from the internet, a movie, or one of their friends at school. We saw it as our responsibility to invest in their lives and in their future marriage.

Master "Sweet"
The master bedroom should be the most sacred place in the house. It should be a room filled with sweetness, a sanctuary from the hectic world where the husband and wife can rest, re-

lax, unwind, and even play. In order for the master bedroom to become this kind of haven, it needs to be a safe place – a place where nakedness isn't just physical, but also emotional and spiritual. Great sex isn't just a physical act. In fact, it is deep, satisfying, and intimate when it is the consummation of a relationship that is transparent, honest, and genuine.

The master bedroom in our house is the most special room in our home. It is not a room with piles of laundry on the floor, overflowing trash, or a constantly unmade bed. We (and by "we" I mean "mainly Candy") keep it picked up, clean and fresh. It has candles, a sound system with romantic CDs close at hand, along with special lighting for our intimate moments together. Since Candy is "freezing" whenever the temperature dips below 70 degrees, I installed a corner fireplace in our room. Along with supplying the necessary heat, it also provides its own romantic ambience.

One of the choices we made when we first got married was to not have a television in our bedroom. I knew myself well enough to know that I'd stay up watching the same highlights on ESPN over and over again, to the detriment of our married life. Plus, when it was time to go to bed I wanted to sleep with my wife, not a remote! Now Candy and I often slip away upstairs to our master suite to watch a movie together on our portable DVD player, but we've chosen to guard our bedroom from anything that could hinder our marriage or intimacy.

Fox Hunting

I am not a hunter. Although I enjoy the beauty of mountains and forest, I am completely comfortable in an urban setting with concrete, freeways, and noise. And, since God has a sense of humor, He put me in the Great Northwest and surrounded me with hunters.

One of my best friends is Paul Hill. His main responsibilities as my executive pastor are to keep me out of trouble and try to figure out a way to find money for all of the ministry ideas that pop into my head. Paul has been a hunter ever since he began following his father into the forest as a young boy. His home isn't really what I'd call a normal house – it's more like a hunting lodge. His wife, Kassi, is cool enough to allow Paul to mount his wild game trophies all throughout their home. On his walls are deer, ducks, elk, coyotes, and this enormous moose! He even has a bear skin on the floor. I have to resist the urge to grunt and pound my chest whenever I'm at his house. Between Paul and the other hunters in my church, I've gotten plenty of invitations to join them in their hunting escapades. I've turned them down every time, though – I don't want to risk never having sex again with a wife who won't look at me because *I killed Bambi!*

But from another perspective, I *am* a hunter and I have been hunting for the past quarter century. In fact, my wife actually hunts with me! We hunt foxes. They are not real foxes, but symbolic ones which prey upon every marriage.

In the Song of Solomon we see the woman saying to her beloved,

> *"Catch for us the foxes, the little foxes that ruin the vineyards, our vineyards that are in bloom."* (2:15)

Every marriage has foxes, little foxes that represent obstacles or temptations that have plagued every marriage since Adam and Eve in the Garden of Eden. These destructive animals will destroy the vineyard of romance, trust, and respect if they are not constantly hunted and killed. This kind of hunting is not seasonal. It is year-round!

In this verse the woman is asking the man to take the initiative in hunting these foxes. In a healthy marriage, the husband will take leadership in their relationship. This provides her the security of knowing that her husband is taking their relationship seriously and making efforts to protect it.

One of the foxes we all need to hunt is the one called *Selfishness*. This critter will destroy any relationship. Many people mistakenly identify hatred as the opposite of love. It isn't. Selfishness is the opposite of love. Love is giving – selfishness is taking. Love is sacrificial – selfishness wants the other person to sacrifice. Love thinks of the other person – selfishness is consumed with themselves.

Selfishness in the master bedroom is destructive. It can show up when you shut down your spouse when they want and need your physical attention. It can also manifest itself if you become a demanding partner who indulges in unhealthy fantasies or uncontrolled lust. This kind of behavior will drive a wedge between the married couple, becoming a "little fox" that will damage any romantic vineyard.

Other foxes are called *Bitterness* and *Resentment*. Sometimes these foxes begin like a little pebble in your shoe, tiny annoyances that will grow over time if they are not dealt with. These foxes can also be born out of hurtful comments or neglect that damage trust and intimacy.

Every relationship will try your soul over time. That's what fallen and sinful people do to each other, including the people we love the most. If we are not careful, we can end up taking our spouse for granted and little irritations begin to grow. Partners in a healthy marriage will be quick to communicate when they've been hurt, and quick to forgive. We've all been guilty of saying things that come out wrong and cause pain. There will be times when we let our spouse down and fail them. A healthy marriage will be quick to resolve conflict and seek restoration.

Although it is possible to have sex when there is bitterness or resentment in the relationship, it is impossible to have deep, passionate intimacy when the marriage is in this damaged state. The Bible warns us,

"Do not let the sun go down while you are still angry, and do not give the devil a foothold." (Ephesians 4:26-27)

I remember nights where my wife and I were both pretending to be asleep, knowing that there was unresolved conflict between us. Eventually one of us would surrender the pathetic ground we were fighting for, and make the choice to resolve and forgive. Forgiveness would lead to restoration, and sometimes restoration would even lead to intimacy in the early hours.

The foxes of bitterness and resentment can creep up on you. If we are not vigilant, these invasive pests can ruin acres of precious ground in our marriages.

Another fox that can destroy a marriage is the fox of *Discontentment*. "If he would only make more money," she thinks to herself. "If she would only lose some weight," he counters. Destructive. Deadly.

This fox can often be allowed into the marriage when a husband fantasizes about other women. He begins to think to himself, "Why can't my wife look like that?" How unfair and unrealistic it is to measure our wives against women who are airbrushed and surgically enhanced.

Another way this fox makes its way into a man's heart is by the subtle seeds our culture plants via commercials, movies, and other forms of advertisement. Take a closer look at some of the commercials being televised today. Many times the woman is portrayed as the aggressive pursuer of the man. In one commercial advertising a new and improved razor, we see an attractive woman pushing her guy into a chair, ripping off her top, and tossing it in his face. Many movie trailers display a hot leading lady aggressively forcing herself onto the man and initiating a passionate kiss. This can plant a seed of discontent in the heart of a man, leading him to think, "Why doesn't my wife kiss me like that?"

On the flip side, the fox of discontentment can wedge its way into the heart of a woman when she romanticizes the men in chick flicks or romance novels. She begins to size up her man with the Matthew McConaugheys of the Hollywood version of reality and thinks, "Why can't my husband talk to me or treat me like this?" In reality, no man can measure up to Matthew McConaughey, not even Matthew McConaughey! On the other hand, I bet I *could* be that romantic if I had a handful of script writers helping me out! Most counselors will tell you that affairs often do not begin for sexual reasons – they begin for emotional reasons. The fox of discontentment is emotionally based. We kill this fox with realistic expectations, truth, and a thankful heart.

On the walls of our master bedroom are mounted the invisible carcasses of the "foxes" that Candy and I have hunted and killed. We mount new ones all the time, because this kind of hunting season does not end. We know that if we stop hunting, we could damage the marriage we hold so dear.

The master bedroom of our homes needs constant attention. Do not let selfishness, bitterness, resentment, or discontentment gain a foothold in this room. Continue to invest in the physical aspect of your marriage so that intimacy, pure intimacy, will be a hallmark of your marriage. Invest in your marriage by going on dates, attending marriage conferences, and reading resources that will help keep the fire lit in your marriage. A healthy and happy master suite will go a long way toward making your home stay healthy and happy.

Small Group Questions:

1. How was sex taught to you when you were growing up? Is your view of sex in alignment with God's view of sex?

2. How has your church helped or not helped your family with its teaching on the subject of sex?

3. How do you and your spouse provide a healthy model for your children of a husband and wife who are in love with each other? Are you uncomfortable showing physical affection with each other in the presence of your children? If so, why?

4. How often do you and your spouse go out on dates? If you are not in a regular habit of dating, what are your reasons? What are your dating habits demonstrating to your children?

5. What foxes need to be hunted in your marriage? Which foxes are the most challenging for your and your spouse to hunt? Why?

"Discipline doesn't break a child's spirit half as often as the lack of it breaks a parent's heart."
Unknown

Chapter Seven
The Laundry Room: Discipline

The laundry room is one of those necessary evils in every home. We all know we need a place to clean the dirt and grime from our clothes, but few people get all that excited about actually *doing* laundry.

The door to the laundry room is the one that always gets closed when guests come over. When we're giving a tour of the house, this is the room we skip. It's a room we'd like everybody else to ignore, but if we have any plans to go out in public, this room is important if we don't want to wear clothes that stink to high heaven.

In our imaginary dream house, the laundry room symbolizes discipline. Without discipline, we risk sending our kids out in public with a "smell" that's impossible to ignore. Without discipline, our kids will have stained and soiled behavior that makes other people want to avoid them. Loving parents choose to discipline their children, and ideally, they are mature enough to take care of it in private, instead of airing their "dirty laundry" to the world. Discipline is a necessary evil (or at least it *feels* like an "evil" sometimes) that must take place if a home is to be truly healthy and happy.

Many kids don't like hauling their clothes down to the laundry room. If you have boys, their favorite shirt has to be practically dripping with mud before they'll even acknowledge that it's dirty. If your girls are like mine, they'd much rather pile up their dirty clothes in their closet or in the corner of the bathroom until there's nothing left in their closet but a swimsuit, a down parka, and three mismatched socks. This dire situation finally forces them to drag their clothes into the laundry room.

Why is this? There are just so many other things we'd rather do than the simple but mundane chore of washing our clothes, folding them, and restocking the dresser drawers. As a child, the torturous chore I dreaded the most each Saturday was laundry. My mom made us kids sort, fold, and stack the laundry in our family room. With a family of nine, the pile of clothes seemed like a mountain to me. This laborious task felt like it took *forever*, and just when I thought I was done, my mom would drop another basket full of clothes in the middle of the floor. Ugh!

But if you think laundry is a traumatic experience for you, consider it from the perspective of your clothes! First, you're thrown into a pile with other smelly garments, and you remain there for days or weeks. Then you're tossed into a machine full of freezing cold or scalding hot water. You're tossed back and forth as cleaning solutions are poured into the tank. After a while, you're spinning around in circles, pinned against the outer wall doing a hundred G's. Then you're unceremoniously tossed into another machine where you're blasted with hot air and tumbled around until you're dry. And heaven help you if you've got a stain ... you're doused in chemicals, abandoned to soak, scrubbed to within an inch of your life, and THEN you go in the wash! It seems harsh, unfair, and cruel.

Children can view discipline the same way. The fact is, whoever is doing laundry isn't being mean to the clothes. We are not trying to hurt the clothes or ruin them – we are trying to properly care for these delicate fabrics, since they are valuable and worth saving. Failing to consistently wash and care for our clothes will cause them to wear out prematurely. In the same way, parents who consistently discipline their children are not trying to be mean or cruel – they are properly caring for them, because they love them.

Important Clarification

Before I lose anyone right out of the gate, let me explain what I am *not* talking about. I am not talking about beating your child, child endangerment, or abuse. I will state this here and restate it later – any punishment administered to a child out of anger is inappropriate, out of bounds, and potentially abusive! What I am talking about is healthy, loving, and consistent disciplining of a child.

The challenge today is that we live in a culture that strives to protect our children, at all costs, from any and all pain. Some of this is healthy – I'm thankful for inventions like seat belts, booster seats, gates for stairs, and childproof caps on medicine. After all, good parents want to provide a safe physical environment for the children they love.

However, there are many young parents today who are a product of what I call the "Pampered Generation." They learned how to ride a bike under OSHA-approved attire consisting of bike helmets, elbow pads, knee pads, and butt pads. All scrapes and boo-boo's were eliminated with this full-body protective armor. This generation also grew up with sporting events where scores were not kept, because someone might lose. Everyone on every team received a trophy, no matter what place the team finished. There was virtually no way to hold a child back a grade due to poor grades. Any thought of hurting a child's feelings was anathema. Many of this generation are now parents, and it can't help but affect the way they raise their own children.

Even with the best intentions, the pendulum of safety can swing in an unhealthy direction if we are not careful. Don't get me wrong – I am all for protecting the physical well-being of children. However, it is unhealthy and harmful when children are protected from the natural consequences of their poor decisions. This is evident in a home where discipline is rare or inconsistent.

My parents loved me enough to use the laundry room of discipline with me, early and often. Whenever I chose the path of disobedience or disrespect, I forced my parents to make choices of their own in response to my bad decisions. Their response was often to apply what they called the "Board of Education" to my "Seat of Learning." As I got older, discipline involved a loss of privileges or freedom. I was not physically harmed or emotionally damaged in any way – in fact, the opposite was true. My laundry room experience reinforced the healthy boundaries my parents gave me. It also taught me that crime (disobedience or disrespect) did not pay!

In this chapter, I want to give you some blueprints for discipline that will benefit your child, your home, and your sanity. My goal is for parents to realize that discipline can be a very positive thing in the life and well-being of a child.

The Goal of Parenting

Before we talk about the challenges and principles of disciplining our children, let's back up a little – we must establish the goal of our parenting. Every parent is on a path of parenting, and it's going to lead *somewhere!* If we have no goal in mind, that path may wind up in the rocks and weeds, with our children stumbling through life far from where they ought to be. Having the destination in mind helps keep us focused and on track. As with everything else in life, if we don't have a goal, we will wander around aimlessly, wasting valuable time and energy in the process. As parents, we don't have time or energy to waste.

Andy Stanley's book *The Principle of the Path* addresses this issue. The Principle of the Path is simple: "Direction, not intention, determines destination."[6]

Interstate 5 runs north and south along the entire west coast of the United States, spanning Washington, Oregon and California. If Candy and I decide to take the kids to Disneyland for our family vacation, we'll have to take I-5 South from our home in Washington State in order to reach the magical kingdom. If we plan the trip, pack our bags, gas up the car, and then hop on the freeway heading north, we will never reach Disneyland. It won't matter what our intentions are. It won't matter if we pray about our trip beforehand or if we listen to the Christian radio station while we're happily driving our car straight to Canada. Northbound Interstate 5 will *never* get us to Disneyland. Our direction determines our destination, every time!

What is your goal as a parent? Whether you realize it or not, you are on a parenting path that will have an eventual destination. Where will this path take you? Where will this path take your children when they arrive at adulthood? Do your daily parenting decisions lead you in that direction?

Where our girls were young, Candy and I sat down together and talked about the pattern we saw all too often, in which parents were driven to see their children succeed in sports, academics, and other pursuits. We realized that more than any of these positive but temporary things, we wanted our children to have strong character, and we made a parenting goal that reflected this desire. Simply stated, this is what we came up with: *We want to provide training and tools for our children in order for them to be responsible adults with character and a genuine love for God.* Time will tell whether we reach this destination, but we are determined to do our part as parents in charting this path for our girls.

Our hope is that when they head off to college, their roommates will be able to say, "I have a responsible roommate with awesome character, and she genuinely loves God." When our girls are in the workplace, we want their employers to think, whether consciously or subconsciously, "This is a great employee that I can really depend on. She's honest and hardworking, and I get the impression she's religious." There will come a day when a young man will ask for my blessing to marry one of my daughters. After he turns in his 37-page application and the $10,000 application fee, I hope to hear, "I love your daughter so much. She is the most amazing woman I have ever met. I love her heart, her character, and her love for God."

My girls will not arrive at this destination by accident. Rarely does any child stumble upon this kind of success by chance. I believe it is the parents' responsibility to provide the necessary training and tools to help each of their children reach great destinations in adulthood. This process begins with establishing clearly defined boundaries for their children.

Boundaries

Every good parent provides clear boundaries for their children. When a child grows up with non-existent or inconsistent boundaries they will develop insecurities and destructive habits. Without boundaries and the necessary consequences when these boundaries are violated, parents set their children up for failure in life.

Each summer, our family enjoys packing our food, catching the ferry, and walking to Safeco Field to watch the Seattle Mariners play baseball. We always arrive early for batting practice, hoping to catch a baseball that sails into the outfield seats. After batting practice, the field is cleared and the grounds crews begin the tedious work that must be completed before the umpire's call of "play ball" can echo through the stadium. Several crews begin raking the warning track and infield dirt. Then they water it so that there is minimal dust during the game. Meanwhile, another crew begins chalking the foul lines, base paths, and batter's box.

These boundary lines are chalked before every game, even if the chalk lines from the previous game are still visible. The crews aren't chalking the lines according to how they're feeling that day, nor are they making a best-guess estimate on the lines' placement. Instead, these lines are carefully measured and clearly marked according to the *Official Baseball Rules*, the manual used by every Major League team. Bases are then placed within the baselines in the same predictable places so runners don't have to guess where the bases will be while they're running the base paths. These baseball boundary lines are precise, predictable, and consistent.

Imagine what would happen if these lines were random and inconsistent. Imagine if these boundary lines moved and shifted throughout the game. Can you picture the pandemonium that would result if the bases were moved in between innings and repositioned somewhere in the outfield? The result would be disastrous! There would be confusion and chaos, which would soon give way to arguments and fights. Eventually the players would quit out of sheer frustration.

God knows that life works better when we have boundary lines. He knows that boundary lines provide protection and security. Even in a perfect environment, the Garden of Eden, we see God setting some boundary lines for Adam.

> *"The Lord God took the man and put him in the Garden of Eden to work it and take care of it. And the Lord commanded the man, 'You are free to eat from any tree in the garden; but you must not eat from the tree of the knowledge of good and evil, for when you eat of it you will surely die.'" (Genesis 2:15-17)*

God's chalk line was clear: Eat from any of the many trees in the garden. Enjoy the fruit of all the trees in fair territory – knock yourselves out, kids! But there is one tree, just one tree, which is off limits to you. The tree of the knowledge of good and evil is out of bounds.

There are many other examples of God's chalk lines in Scripture. The Ten Commandments – chalk lines. Marriage roles, family roles, and church roles in the New Testament – chalk lines. When Jesus said, "I am the way, the truth and the life. No one comes to the Father except through me" (John 14:6), that was another clearly marked line.

God's boundary lines help us determine what is foul or fair territory in life. They're not there as a result of divine cruelty, but rather are given to us by a loving Heavenly Father who wants to protect His children. God didn't draw the line around the tree of the knowledge of good and evil to taunt Adam and Eve, but to protect them from a world of hurt, evil, and pain.

Adam and Eve chose to ignore the boundaries God had clearly established for them. Instead, they listened to the serpent and ate from the forbidden tree. Instantly, the pristine Garden of Eden began to smell of sin, and their relationship with God was stained. If God had ignored the stench and the filth of their sin, He would have ceased to be a holy God. Instead, God took Adam and Eve to the metaphorical laundry room, and consequences were given. Unfortunately, the stain from their disobedience was passed on to every living person after them. Thankfully, the stain of sin was eventually scrubbed clean by the death of Jesus Christ on the cross.

Chalk Lines

Here are some examples of the chalk lines that Candy and I have laid down in our home. These boundaries have been chalked and re-chalked over the years to continually reflect the parenting goal we mentioned earlier. As you will notice, we chose not to have too many lines. The more boundary lines you set, the more difficult they are to maintain.

Respect

The chalk line between respect (fair ball) and disrespect (foul ball) will help our children in every area of their life. Respect is seen in the ways they respond to their parents, grandparents, siblings, teachers, coaches, police, and other authority figures. It is revealed in their attitudes, choices, and language. Respect (or lack of it) is evident in the tone and tenor of their voice, in their facial expressions, and in their body language.

If children do not learn to respect their parents, how can we expect them to respect other people in authority as they grow older? If parents do not teach respect, model it, and expect their children to have respect for those around them, their children will travel through life with a stench that will permeate every relationship.

Trust

The line between trust (fair) and distrust (foul) helps to determine the quality of life and freedom our children will enjoy in our home and beyond. If I can trust my child to be honest and up-front with me, life will go well for them and they'll gain more freedom from their mom and from me. If they're being dishonest or shading the truth in order to avoid getting into hot water, I'll limit their freedom and make their life uncomfortable. Without the boundary line of trust, their life and future will be filled with difficulty and trouble. A lack of trust is a deep-seated stain that must be addressed before it settles into the fabric of their character. However, helping our children become people whom others can trust will set them up to be a sweet aroma to everyone they associate with.

Responsibility

The chalk line between responsibility (fair) and irresponsibility (foul) will be a measure of maturity in their life, both now and in adulthood. Our children realized at an early age that they were a part of what I call the "Bandara Work Release Program." Simply put, if they help with the work, they can be released.

Being a part of the Bandara family involves contributing to our family. Chores and helping around the house are not optional. When my daughters are contributing members of our family, it makes it easier for me to say "yes" when they ask if they can go to the mall, meet their friends at Starbucks, catch a movie, or have a sleepover. If they do the work, they are free to go. If they don't do the work, the answer is a calm but non-negotiable "No." I joke with my girls, "I work for the food, Mom shops for and cooks the food, and you work to eat the food."

The chalk line of responsibility helps kids to develop maturity and a good work ethic that will sustain them the rest of their lives.

Opposite Sex Relationships

Some parents leave it up to their children to decide where the "foul lines" are when it comes to their relationships with the opposite sex. I firmly believe that telling a adolescent full of colliding hormones to "follow their heart" with the opposite sex is foolish, naïve, and maybe just plain stupid. I have seen too many teenagers follow their hearts right off the cliff of sexually transmitted disease. I believe our kids need boundaries (or electric fences, if necessary!) in this important area of life in order to help them navigate this emotionally challenging time. Parents, we have already been down this road. We know what to expect. We know the pitfalls. We can help.

Since your child's teen years *are* coming, ready or not, the best time to set the boundaries in this area is before the child reaches adolescence. Candy and I purposefully told our girls, while our girls were still young enough to think boys were yucky, that they would one day be attracted to boys. They rolled their eyes at us and gave us the "you guys are totally crazy" look. They later realized that their parents could actually predict the future.

Years before any of my daughters were old enough to go on dates, I chalked a boundary line that they couldn't go out on one-on-one dates until they were at least sixteen. My student ministry experience had told me that single dating in early adolescence is dangerous and unwise. In addition to this, for their benefit and protection, I chalked an extra line – before any guy asked her out, the guy must first ask me for permission.

The day I first gave this boundary line to one of my daughters, she looked at me with an expression that said, "Why in the world would I ever want to be alone with a boy?" Occasionally I would remind her of this guideline, even as she rolled her eyes at me in the universal pre-teen code for "Whatever." I knew, however, that this day would come. To prepare myself for this inevitable day, I read Dennis Rainey's excellent book, *Interviewing My Daughter's Date*. (Great read, dads!)

Several years later I was talking with my friend Tony after church when someone tapped me on the shoulder. [Note: All names in this section have been changed to protect the innocent.] I turned and saw a pale teenaged guy standing next to me. When I asked him how I could help him, he said, "Hello, my name is Steve. I was wondering if I could ask your daughter out for Homecoming." I responded calmly, "Sit here and let me finish my conversation and then we can talk." He sat down nervously. I whispered to Tony, "The day is finally here! Let's talk a little more and make him wait!"

I finished up with Tony, and then spent some time interviewing Steve to find out why he wanted to ask my daughter out, and what the particulars were for this date. I then took the opportunity to inform him what he could do and couldn't do with my daughter. I wanted him to know where the chalk lines were, and exactly what was going to be considered fair and foul. He was very respectful, and I appreciated him looking me in the eye and letting me know how he was going to take care of my most important investment: my daughter! By the end of our conversation his normal color had returned. I asked him how he was doing and he answered, "This wasn't as hard as I first thought. At least you aren't the kind of father who owns a gun!" I laughed and replied, "But I do own a baseball bat!" Steve and my daughter had a great time together, and they remain good friends to this day.

A few months later another young man, John, wanted to talk with me to ask if he could date this same daughter. As I was interviewing him in our backyard on a beautiful August day, I didn't realize that all three of my girls were upstairs taking advantage of the location of Ashley's bedroom window, trying to listen to our conversation below! I had a great time with John as we talked about his standards and mine. I explained how I wanted him to respect and protect my daughter. I helped him see that one day my daughter would be a wife, and that her behavior in all her previous relationships would need to be an open book to the man she married. This time with John gave me a great opportunity to communicate my boundary lines, along with my three challenges to him: Respect her, protect her, and honor her.

Later that afternoon, I spent some time with my daughter apart from the rest of the family. I shared with her all that I'd talked about with John so that she would know that I hadn't said or done anything that would be embarrassing. When we were done talking, I asked her, "How does it make you feel to hear all of this?" She responded, "It makes me feel so special." Exactly!

For several months they dated as boyfriend and girlfriend. During their time together, he treated her like a princess and my daughter learned how to properly respond to a guy. We enjoyed having him as a part of our family in that time. Before going off to college they returned to being just friends, but the end result was something highly unusual among their peers: They left as better friends than when they started dating. The boundary lines that were set for them could have easily been disregarded. They chose to honor them, and because of that they remain friends with a healthy mutual respect for each other.

Consequences

Chalk lines or boundaries of behavior, no matter how clearly they are marked, are absolutely meaningless if they are not enforced. Parents must learn to be good "umpires" in their homes. It may not be popular, convenient, or fun, but somebody has to enforce the rules or chaos will ensue.

We saw how God clearly chalked a boundary line for Adam in Genesis 2:15-17. God was clear and concise with His boundary line for the one off-limits tree in the Garden of Eden. However, in Genesis 3 we see that Adam and Eve knowingly crossed that line and ate from the tree of the knowledge of good and evil. Eve was deceived, and Adam knowingly disobeyed. With all the freedom given to them to eat from any of the trees in the garden except one, they still chose not to control themselves, and they fell into sin. And we wonder where our kids get this!

God had a choice: To enforce his boundary line or to ignore it. God chose to lovingly but firmly enforce the line He had chalked. In Genesis 3:6-17 we see God modeling three keys to good discipline in the way that He brought consequences to bear for Adam and Eve's disobedience.

Three Keys to Good Discipline
Be Consistent

Being consistent is almost always the most difficult part of discipline for parents. There are so many factors that work against us – we're physically fatigued, emotionally drained, distracted by everyday life, and tired of enforcing the same guidelines over and over again. Regardless, if we are not consistent in our enforcement of the boundary lines, we are asking for major trouble.

Being a consistent parent can make you feel like you're on constant border patrol. Do you ever feel like Bill Murray in *Groundhog Day* as you correct the same infraction day after day? Being truly consistent as a parent means that talking back is consistently corrected, disobedience is consistently dealt with, and disrespect is consistently punished. Being consistent means that throwing a tantrum is never acceptable, lying is never tolerated, and both are dealt with swiftly. Being consistent communicates to our children that we mean what we say and say what we mean. Being consistent is training our children that our "yes" means "yes" and our "no" means exactly that – "no."

The best umpires in baseball are the ones who are the most consistent. Major league players and managers understand that there are no perfect umpires. Mistakes will be made because of the human factor involved. The same can be said about parents. There are no perfect parents. Our children know and understand this. But the best parents are the ones who are the most consistent.

For umpires, the key to consistency is ensuring that they are in a good position to see the play in order to make the right call. They can't be out of position, with a player obstructing their view of the play. Parents also need to be in the right position emotionally, physically, and spiritually so that we can make the right call with our children. That is why it is important that we take care of our physical health, strive to be emotionally balanced, and maintain our own spiritual well-being. However, even if parents are in the right position to make the right call with their children, they can still sometimes get it wrong.

A perfect game in baseball is one without a hit, error, or walk in the game. It means that 27 players come up to bat, and 27 players get out. On June 2, 2010, Detroit Tigers pitcher Armando Galarraga was pitching a perfect game into the bottom of the ninth inning. So far 26 players had come to the plate and 26 players had gotten out. Now Armando was facing the 27th player, Jason Donald of the Cleveland Indians. Donald hit a grounder to the right side of the infield between first and second base. The ball wasn't hit too hard and first basemen Miguel Cabrera was able to get over to it and throw it to Galarraga, who was running over to cover first base. Galarraga caught the ball and touched first base. In full speed, it looked close but it still appeared that Donald was out. The initial celebration for a perfect game came to a shocking end as the first base umpire, Jim Joyce, called Donald safe. The perfect game was over.

Jim Joyce was convinced that he had made the right call. But upon seeing the replay after the game, Joyce clearly saw what everyone else had seen on TV. The runner was out by a half step. Joyce was devastated. He then made a decision that you rarely see in baseball. He immediately made a public apology for making the wrong call. Jim admitted his mistake and declared to the media, "I cost that kid a perfect game."

The next day the same two teams were playing, and Jim was now the umpire behind the plate. The home plate umpire is the one who receives the lineup cards from the team's manager or designated player before the game. Detroit's manager chose to have Armando Galarraga bring out the Tigers lineup card. It was a touching scene at home plate when Jim Joyce and Galarraga met and shook hands. Jim began to tear up as he personally apologized to Armando. The reaction of the fans watching this scene was incredible. Instead of booing the umpire whose blown call cost Galarraga a perfect game, they began to cheer. They cheered because of how Joyce humbly and authentically owned up to his mistake.

We know we don't always get it right 100% of the time, and our kids aren't oblivious to this fact. I've been guilty of falsely accusing one of my children, and I've even gone so far as to actually punish the wrong child. When she was saying, "Daddy, it wasn't me," I came back with, "Don't talk back." Upon realizing my mistake, I had to apologize and ask for her forgiveness.

It is not imperfection that frustrates our children the most, though – it is inconsistency. When the chalk lines are ignored in one instance and then rigorously enforced in the next, this confuses our children. When parents are hard on one child and go easy on another for the same offense, this can plant the seed of bitterness in the heart of the child who received the harsher treatment.

God demonstrated consistency in the Garden with Adam and Eve when He followed through with punishment when they crossed the boundary line. He had promised them that they would die as punishment. Death immediately crept into their relationship with God, and they found themselves running for cover from Him. Although they didn't realize it, Adam and Eve began to physically die at the moment of disobedience. Soon afterward, God would banish them from the Garden of Eden. God was consistent with His Word.

It has been years since I've had to spank one of my children. Yes, I said "spanked." I lovingly applied the "Board of Education" to their "Seat of Learning" when they chose to disobey, just like my parents did with me. I believe Proverbs 22:15 when it says, "Foolishness is bound up in the heart of a child, but the rod of discipline will drive it far from him" (NASB). We found that applying a little pain to the bottom (a reason God provides extra padding there) would often trigger the right response the next time they wanted to disobey.

Here is the process we used: We would explain why we were disciplining them, and then we would spank them with a little wooden spoon. (I believe that the open hand is for showing affection, not for disciplining.) Then we would hug them and hold them, and finally pray with them.

One of my girls is strong-willed and was spanked on a regular basis when she was young. I could count on her to provide plenty of drama whenever the smallest amount of pain was applied to her bottom. Another child of mine would receive a spanking and give me a look that said, "Was that supposed to hurt, or did a fly land on me?" We had to look at other avenues of punishment to get her attention. My youngest daughter didn't get spanked as much as her sisters. It wasn't a case of favoritism – it was simply that she has a very tender heart and would respond quickly to any sort of confrontation or raised voice. Immediately she would tear up and begin singing the hymn, "I Surrender All."

Other forms of discipline would be the temporary suspension of privileges such as access to the TV, computer, video games, phones, iPods, etc. Other effective consequences may include extra chores, cancelled outings, or calling their coach to explain why they can't be at the next practice or game. Ouch!

We still discipline our girls today, but there is very little drama now. That's because Candy and I did the hard work while they were young, remaining consistent time and time again. Now our girls usually respond quickly and appropriately with very little pushback. Why? They were trained repeatedly that the chalk lines were there for a reason, and would be enforced consistently.

Although they still dislike the "laundry room" of discipline, they are now old enough to see (and smell) what happens when their friends are allowed to display behavior that stinks to high heaven without the consistent cleaning and scrubbing that discipline provides.

Be Clear

If consistency is the most difficult part of discipline, being clear is the most overlooked part of discipline. Parents often assume that their children know why the chalk lines are there. I don't have to tell you what happens when we assume, do I?

God was very clear when He laid down the chalk line regarding the tree of the knowledge of good and evil. He was very clear about what the punishment would be if the line was crossed. He clearly communicated His expectations beforehand.

After Adam and Eve disobeyed, we find God asking them four questions before He dispensed His discipline. He asked them, *"Where are you?"* (3:9) When they responded by saying that they were hiding because they were naked, God asked, *"Who told you that you were naked?"* (3:11a) He then asked them, *"Have you eaten from the tree that I commanded you not to eat from?"* (3:11b) Later He says, *"What is this you have done?"* (3:13)

It is wise for parents to ask their kids questions when they have disobeyed. Asking questions reminds our children of the clear boundaries we've set, and helps drive home the strong biblical role of the parent. Just as God made Adam and Eve answer for their disobedience, our children should verbalize theirs. It makes an impression in their hearts when they have to put into their own words what they have done wrong.

Before Adam and Eve receive their punishment, God does something simple but powerful when He says, *"Because you have done this..."* (3:14, 17) God reminds them why they are being disciplined. This reinforces the chalk lines, focusing the attention on the boundary line, rather than on the person enforcing the boundary line.

I came across an equation that has greatly helped me in ministry and as a parent: *High Expectations + Clear Instructions = Quality.* Having high expectations is not bad. Having unrealistic expectations *is.* I expect certain behavior and results from my children, and they understand this. It is our responsibility as parents, however, to give clear instructions for how our children are supposed to meet our expectations. I have found that most children *want* to please their parents. If we give them the "how" they will usually rise to the challenge and succeed. When we first assigned our girls the responsibility of cleaning their bathroom, Candy cleaned it with them to show them exactly what "clean" means to us. The high expectation was accompanied by clear instruction.

Our girls love doing things with their friends. We tell them, "You can go, but your chores must be finished before you leave." Each week Candy posts on a whiteboard which girl is responsible for which chores each week. The whiteboard clearly lays out who is in charge of feeding the dog, cleaning the kitchen, taking care of the dishwasher, etc. They know the expectations and necessary instructions. Ashley liked receiving her allowance, but she knew her bank account must be balanced first before she received her money. This required us to teach her how to balance her checking account. High Expectations + Clear Instruction = Quality.

All children have a propensity to push the boundary lines. All children instinctively know which parent they can "work" –

that is, manipulate emotionally. They can sense which parent will make them eat their vegetables and which one will be a softy for ice cream. They somehow know these things before they can even speak a full sentence. But what they really need to know is what will happen when they cross that line!

Being consistent and being clear will help parents with the emotions that naturally surface in the heat of disobedience.

Be Calm

The best umpires are calm. They call a strike, an out, or a foul ball with little to no emotion. They see the call and make the call. When the manager comes running out from the dugout with steam rising from his head and spit flying from his mouth, and gets about three inches from the umpire's face, the best umpires just stand there calmly. Even if the manager crosses the line and says the magic words (usually certain swear words) that force umpires to toss the manager out of the game, they simply toss them. Then they calmly walk back to their umpiring position on the field.

I have never seen an umpire call a foul ball, yell at the batter, "How many times do I have to tell you, keep it fair, okay?", and start crying. I have also never seen an umpire call a strike three and follow the batter back to the dugout, yelling after him, "Go back and sit down and think about what you just did!"

I realize that emotions in the midst of a conflict at home are real and often painful. I look back on a period of my life when I was a poor parent because I wasn't in control of my emotions. I'd get angry and yell in a very loud voice, thinking, "If I yell louder it will make the punishment more effective." How foolish! When I was out of control emotionally, it made everything worse.

I still carry deep regret about what I am about to share with you. One night about ten years ago, I was stressed and impatient with life. One of my daughters spoke disrespectfully to her mother, and I lost it. I still have images in my mind's eye of her running to her room while I was yelling at her. I chased after her. She jumped in her bed and covered herself with her blankets. As I yanked back the covers, I discovered a daughter who was terrified, not of her punishment, but of her father. The fear in her eyes brought me to tears then, and it still does today as I write this. Thankfully I didn't lay a hand on her in my anger. In fact, that night I didn't punish her at all. I punished *myself*, because the line she crossed in disobedience paled in comparison to the line I crossed in anger. Thankfully she forgave me when I tearfully asked for her forgiveness.

As I said before, never punish your child when you are angry. Never! It can all too quickly cross that invisible line between appropriate discipline and abuse. It will leave emotional scars that can take years to heal. Sometimes they never heal.

God, once again, teaches us by example how to maintain our emotional control when we are disciplining our children. In our story from Genesis, it says,

> *"Then the man and his wife heard the sound of the Lord God as he was **walking** in the garden in the cool of the day..." (Genesis 3:8, emphasis mine)*

God gives no indication that He was angry. God could have lit up the sky with lighting and thunder, with a little fire and brimstone thrown in as well. While that would have been impressive, God chose instead to "walk." Not run, but walk. Not stomping or crashing through the forest, not making Adam and Eve think the Almighty Bigfoot was coming. He just walked.

God also chose not to show up immediately at the moment of their disobedience. God saw their sin the instant it took place, and He could have appeared on the spot, catching them redhanded with the juice of the fruit still dripping off their chins. Instead, He chose to wait.

We don't know how long God waited, but we know that He came to them in the "cool of the day." He didn't come to them in the heat of the day or the heat of the moment, but later that day.

This is a great example for us as parents. It is so easy for us to respond in the heat of the moment. It is better for us to cool off first before we approach any discipline. This will allow us to calm down, think clearly, and then respond appropriately.

I have found this to be much more effective than acting immediately when I'm emotionally charged. Although I may say the right thing when I'm upset, they will hear the wrong thing in my tone and volume. I may be speaking truth, but in my frustration they will read untruth from my actions. The negative charge will counteract any positive charge of the moment.

Candy and I surprised Holly with a new camera last year. It was the kind of camera that not only takes pictures but has video capability as well. We were tired of Holly borrowing her mother's camera, but we also wanted to reward her for her hard work at school. Several months later I picked Holly up at her friend's house, where I found her in different clothes from the ones she arrived in. Holly and her friends had had a junior high moment and decided to spontaneously jump in the pool, fully clothed. It was a great memory, right up until Holly realized that her camera was in her jeans pocket – which had now just been baptized.

My first reaction was to get upset since I knew I didn't have the money to buy her a new camera. But after a few minutes I calmed myself down and said to her, "I know you were just having fun with your friends. You are not in trouble because it wasn't disobedience, but if you want another camera you will have to pay for it yourself." A couple of years earlier, I would have gone off on her for a long time. Instead, I found that being calm was much more effective. I didn't have to ask her for an apology for my uncontrolled response, and Holly had the wonderful opportunity to work all summer to earn enough money to buy a new camera herself.

During a Christmas break several years ago, Candy and I sat the girls down and told them that we wanted more of their help around the house. Specifically, we wanted them to pick up their stuff instead of leaving it on the stairs, to clean the bathroom more regularly, and to fold their own clothes from the laundry. They all agreed. However, nothing really changed.

Several months later, Candy and I were frustrated with their lack of effort and initiative. They were constantly blaming each other for not helping around the house, and their bathroom was close to being condemned.

Spring break was now upon us, and we gathered the girls together for another family meeting. I told them that their mother and I were tired of asking and reminding them to help around the house. I asked them if they remembered what we had talked about earlier. Yes, they all remembered. Then, I put the ball in their court – I asked them to give themselves a grade on their help and initiative around the house. Each girl, with her head hanging down, mumbled their own grades, ranging from C- to F.

I then explained to them that their mom and I try, within reason, to say "yes" to their requests. Yes to trips to the mall, yes to coffee with friends, yes to birthday parties, sleepovers, etc. Then I said, "For the foreseeable future, without getting upset or emotional, the answer to any and all requests is going to be a simple 'no.'"

At first their response was "Okay, whatever." A few seconds passed, and then reality sank in – *it was only four days until spring break!* Ashley and Holly realized this at the same moment, and it hit Kailey about three seconds later. Sleepovers, trips to the waterfront, plans for friends to come over, all kinds of activities were now in jeopardy. They started asking, "What about this?"

and "What about that?" to which I calmly replied each time, "No." To this one of the girls half-jokingly replied, "It sounds like 'It's the Hard Knock Life!'"

All spring break the answer was an unemotionally delivered "no." Instead of hanging out with their friends, the three of them cleaned the house. Little did Candy and I know that they were also working on a surprise for us while we were at work! At the end of the week they showed off their surprise: They had made a music video of themselves lip-syncing the words to the song from the musical *Annie* called "It's the Hard Knock Life." We all laughed at this hilarious video of them dancing around the house and singing about what mean parents they have. They put it on YouTube and it is still receiving hits to this day!

The Results of Poor Discipline

When parents fail in their responsibility to chalk boundary lines and enforce them in a consistent, clear, and calm way, the results are painful. Parents then force someone else to take responsibility for their irresponsibility.

When parents default on their responsibilities, they leave it up to the school authorities, the police, and their child's future bosses to enforce necessary and healthy boundaries. Parents who have no concept of a laundry room, where behaviors and attitudes are cleaned up and character stains are removed on a regular basis, will set their child up for a harsh reality. Their child will grow up to believe that the world revolves around them, slipping into a life full of excuses to explain away the deficiencies that are evident to everyone around them. They will unwittingly travel through life with smells and stains in their behavior that cause many around them to distance themselves or turn away in quiet disgust.

Failure to provide consistent, clear, and calm discipline at home is a failure to demonstrate love to a child. The Bible gives us time-tested advice when it says,

*"No discipline seems pleasant at the time, but painful.
Later on, however, it produces a harvest of righteousness
and peace for those who have been trained by it."*
(Hebrews 12:11)

I do not believe that a home can be a healthy and happy home without some type of symbolic laundry room – a place where the smells and stains of life can be scrubbed, washed, rinsed, and dried clean. The laundry room experience I had as a child was not fun, but I am so thankful that my parents loved me enough to take me there when I deserved it. I look back with gratitude for parents who saw my future and knew that I needed boundaries in my life if I was going to have any measure of success. I hope my children will look back with the same sense of gratitude for the blueprints of discipline we applied to their lives.

Small Group Questions:

1. Why do many parents avoid disciplining their children?

2. How do you discipline your children when they disobey? What is the most effective form of discipline for each of your children, if you have more than one child?

3. What are some "smells" or "stains" in your children's behavior that need to be cleaned on a consistent basis? What happens if you choose not to clean them?

4. The Principle of the Path says, *"Direction, not intention, determines destination."* What goal (destination) do you have for your children? What are you doing to help them reach this destination?

5. Write down a few examples of major areas in your children's lives that need boundaries. What are the consequences when your children wander into foul territory?

6. If consistency is the most difficult, being clear is the most overlooked, and being calm is the most emotionally challenging part of discipline, which is the area you need the most help in? Why?

7. *"If parents discipline poorly, they will force someone else to take responsibility for their irresponsibility."* What do you think of this statement? What changes, if any, do you need to make in your approach to discipline in your home?

*"We shall neither fail nor falter; we shall not weaken or tire
'give us the tools and we will finish the job."*
Winston Churchill

Chapter Eight
The Man Cave: All the Right Tools

Finally, we come to the garage, which isn't quite like any other room in the house. It's where we store seasonal decorations, personal keepsakes, winter gear, and summer equipment. The garage keeps the weather from ruining valuables like our cars, toys, and bikes. In addition, it's everybody's favorite answer to the question, "Where should I put this?" "I don't know. Put it in the garage for now."

The garage is a part of the house, but not really. It is attached to the house, it's under the same roof as the house, and it adds value to the house, but it isn't included in the home's total square footage. Go figure. Who wants to buy a house without a garage these days? We want a garage when we buy the house, but we're not allowed to count it when we sell the house. Interesting … and confusing!

In recent years the garage has acquired a new name: the Man Cave. Just the sound of this name makes most men want to grunt when they hear it. "The Man Cave" is almost always said in a silly, exaggeratedly deep voice – it sounds cool, manly, and primitive. It indicates that the man of the house has a place to call his own, somewhere he can hide out if he wants to. It signifies that the man is the rightful owner of this part of the domain. No offense, ladies, but the man cave belongs to us men! Urrggh!

Sadly, some view the father's role in the same way that many view the garage. The father is a part of the family, but not really. He lives in the home, kind of. He is there, sort of. In order for a Dream House to become a reality, the father must rise up and take his important place in his home. He is irreplaceable and highly valuable to his entire family. Whenever the father is physically absent or emotionally distant in the home, that home depreciates in value.

Tools

Where do we go when something breaks in the home? The garage! Along with storing stuff and protecting valuables, the garage is where we keep our tools. When something needs strengthening, maintaining, repairing, or replacing, we go to the garage for what we need. The same is true of fathers! Every father has all the tools he needs to strengthen, repair, and maintain health and happiness in his home. It is never too late for fathers to begin using their God-given tools to bless their home.

I believe that nothing compares to the role of the father in the home. Don't get me wrong, mothers are irreplaceable and bring immeasurable value to those who live under their roof. Many mothers leave a tender imprint on the hearts and lives of their children because of their unending love, nurturing, compassion, and help. That's one of the reasons why Mother's Day cards overwhelmingly outsell Father's Day cards. Where would we be without our mothers? With all that said, I believe the father leaves a lasting mark, for better or worse, that is different from all of our other relationships on earth. Like a magnetic pull, every child is subconsciously compelled to please his or her father and gain his acceptance. This powerful need to please Dad continues throughout their lifetime.

In my counseling experience, there's one question that gets to the heart of most issues, and is in fact often the core problem. I ask, "What kind of relationship did you have with your father?" Their reaction usually triggers an immediate and powerful response, depending on the kind of father they experienced.

I've seen anger, tears, and stiff body language from adults who still harbor anger against their fathers. I've also seen grown men and women change before my eyes to reflections of the lost children they once were, with their shoulders sagging and heads lowered as they think back on the roles their fathers played (or didn't play) in their early lives.

God has designed the role of the father to be one of His most effective tools in unveiling His nature to us. In fact, one of the names God gives Himself is "God the *Father*." Because God wants people to have a correct view of Himself, He has given each father the necessary tools to effectively reflect His role as our Heavenly Father. I like to categorize these as Power Tools, Hand Tools, and Precision Tools.

Power Tools

The Apostle Paul pens several interesting descriptions of himself when he writes a letter to the frightened, persecuted first-century believers living in riot-torn Thessalonica. First, he depicts himself as a mother to them.

> *"We were not looking for praise from men, not from you or anyone else. As apostles of Christ we could have been a burden to you, but we were gentle among you, like a mother caring for her little children. We loved you so much that we were delighted to share with you not only the gospel of God but our lives as well, because you had become so dear to us." (I Thessalonians 2:6-8)*

Notice Paul's use of words that are more feminine in nature: *gentle, caring, loved,* and *dear*. I'm not saying that men do not have these qualities, but in general, these words describe many women and most mothers. Paul then illustrates another aspect of his relationship with them a few verses later.

> *"You are witnesses, and so is God, of how holy, righteous and blameless we were among you who believed. For you know that we dealt with each of you as a father deals with*

his own children, encouraging, comforting and urging you to live lives worthy of God, who calls you into his kingdom and glory." (I Thessalonians 2:10-12)

Paul's reminder of his fatherly role was necessary for the growth of the church in Thessalonica. Even two thousand years later, it still serves as a great pattern for every modern-day father to follow in his own home.

The first of three tools Paul mentions is *encouragement*. A more complete definition of the Greek word *parakaleo*, translated as "to encourage," is "to call to one's side; to strengthen; to exhort." If you look on the work bench in the "man cave" of our Dream House, the first thing you'll find is the power tool of encouragement.

Power tools are the loudest tools, the coolest tools, and the tools that bring the biggest change in the shortest amount of time. After a man is finished with a skill saw, power drill, chain saw, belt sander, or leaf blower, he has a sense of satisfaction that a great deal of work has been accomplished much faster than he could have done it unaided. Encouragement has the same effect! It uses the loudest words, the coolest words, and the words that will bring about the biggest change in the shortest amount of time.

In my community of Bremerton, Washington, the largest employer in our county is PSNS – Puget Sound Naval Shipyard, the largest Navy shipyard on the west coast. Bremerton was a hole-in-the-wall community until Pearl Harbor was attacked in 1941. PSNS was called upon to repair many of the damaged ships of the U.S. Fleet and other ships of the Allied Forces throughout World War II. Today, PSNS repairs and refits many of our Navy submarines, ships, and aircraft carriers. Once a year they have a special date set aside when the facility is opened up for tours to the public. On a recent tour I stopped in at one machine shop to get an up-close-and-personal look at what some of the men in my church work on each week. This shop operated very large and very impressive drill presses. These machines are specifically designed to drill through the toughest materials in the world.

When I think of encouragement, the power tool that best describes this attribute is the drill press. Many garages have a drill press, tiny in comparison to the ones they use at the shipyard, but their function is the same. They can drill through hard wood, steel, and iron, leaving behind an indelible impression. The same thing happens with encouragement from a father. These powerful words drill down deep into the heart and leave behind a mark of love that will last for the rest of the child's life. Even the toughest of hearts can eventually be penetrated when a father is determined to encourage his child.

One powerful way to use this tool of encouragement is with the spoken word: It can be a simple affirmation such as "I love you, son" and "You're beautiful, sweetheart." These words can also be related to an achievement or a moment when a child shows strength of character: "I am proud of you!" and "Great job! Keep it up!" Words like these have a way of drilling through the hardened steel of life, bringing light and oxygen into the crevasse of the soul. Don't just think words of encouragement, speak them! Look your son or daughter in the eye and use the drill press of encouragement.

Another Power Tool of Encouragement in a father's tool box is his approval. Communicating your approval will mean more to your children than you may ever realize. Approving words like "I am so glad I have you as a son/daughter" are as valuable as gold, and they're a better long-term investment! Letting your child know that their *best effort* is what matters the most will communicate that your love and approval is not a performance-based exercise.

Stu Weber's book, *Tender Warrior*, is a great book for fathers to read. Stu shares a letter from a woman in his church who experienced an agonizing, lifelong, and desperate search for her father's approval. Here is a portion of her story:

> "My dad was what I thought was a real man. He was the provider and worked hard for our physical needs. He had to go 150 miles away from home to find work, coming home often only on the weekends. As could be expected, I didn't know my dad very well.

> When I reached adolescence, I began to desire more than anything to win his approval. It became an all-consuming need. I went back and forth from being a tomboy to being feminine to try to get him to like me. I took up fishing and made myself pull worms apart and get slime underneath my fingernails so that I could bait my own hooks and we could go fishing. But he didn't have time to go fishing anymore.

> I started playing softball and became the best pitcher in our school. But he never saw me play a game. I worked hard to get straight A's and was always on the honor roll. Never once did he say he was proud of me. One year I was a cheerleader. He never came to a game. One year I was captain of the drill team. He never saw a performance.

> One weekend I tried to help him work on the car. But he was cross with me and I was in the way. I went into the house and made some cookies. He said I baked them too long.

> More and more I found myself retreating to my room on the weekends, sobbing violently, desperately wanting him to care. Not once did he comfort me. He never read to me. He never tucked me into bed. He never hugged me. He never kissed me. He never said, "I love you."

I got married and had four kids. The last one was a boy, the only male descendant. We gave him his name. He wasn't impressed. Restless and dissatisfied with mothering, I went back to school.

Somehow without meaning to, I found myself studying civil engineering, the field of study closest to his profession. I worked as a surveyor last year laying out lines just like the lines he had put in for years. I found myself thinking, "If he could see me now, he would be proud of me."

What a power a father has over the direction of a daughter's life. Good or bad, present or absent, he is going to have an influence that lasts a lifetime. I think a lot of fathers leave their daughters to the mothers to raise, thinking a man's influence isn't necessary for girls.

I'm thirty-seven years old now and beginning to see how much I am still compelled by a deep craving within to gain the approval of this most significant man. You see, if my own father doesn't think I'm worthwhile, I must be worthless. If my own father can't accept me, then I am unacceptable. If my own father cannot love me, then I must be totally unlovable. [7]

Every child has a magnetic pull to seek the approval of their father, no matter how great or how lousy that father may be. A father's approval will bless his children when they are young, and this approval will stay with them for a lifetime. Even after many lost years, a father's approval can begin to slowly cultivate a distant relationship into a more healthy connection with his adult child. It is never too late to start using the Power Tool of Encouragement!

Hand Tools

Next, the Apostle Paul uses the word "comforting" to describe his fatherly role with the church in Thessalonica. This word means "to calm; to console." This is best illustrated by the hand tools found in a garage. Power tools are great, but sometimes a hand tool is more appropriate for a job that needs more finesse and less raw power.

There are all kinds of useful hand tools, like screw drivers, hammers, socket wrenches, or pliers. But when something appears a little off-kilter or just doesn't look right, the one I reach for is a level. This tool has a little bubble in the center that tells me if a picture frame, a shelf, or wall display is accurately level or not. Sometimes the object looks like it's pretty close, if not perfect, and I'm tempted to just leave it as it is. But I double-check it, just in case. Sometimes it looks a little off to my eye, but the level proves that it's straight. However, many times my first instinct is correct, and the level confirms that the object needs to be balanced and readjusted accordingly.

When I was a junior in high school my basketball team finished a successful season and accepted an invitation to a tournament in northern California. Our team played a good tournament, and we defeated our archrival in the championship game. With the crowd and teams eagerly watching, the tournament officials presented the championship trophy to the winning team, and named the All Tournament Team and Most Valuable Player. I knew I had played well in the tournament, but I was so thrilled to have defeated our rival that I wasn't really focused on the award ceremony. When the MVP was announced, I was surprised to hear my name echoing from the speakers. As the applause rumbled from the bleachers, I was thrilled! However, my entire mood changed in an instant from elation to devastation when I witnessed several seniors from my own team shaking their heads in disgust as I made my way past the audience and my teammates to accept my award. I found out later they were hoping that another player, a senior and good friend of mine, would win the award.

All the joy from a great tournament evaporated. As I walked up to receive the trophy, I just wanted a place to hide. I mustered up a fake smile and said "Thank you," but that took everything I had. Of all the trophies I had received over the years, this MVP trophy meant the least to me because of the hurt and rejection I felt from my friends. My father was in the bleachers that day. Although he didn't see what I saw, he knew immediately that something was not right with his son. He instinctively reached for the level.

What I needed most that afternoon was not the power tool of encouragement but the hand tool of comfort. As our team and cheerleaders headed toward the bus to celebrate our victory, my father pulled me aside to ask me if I wanted to ride in his car to the pizza place. He knew exactly what I needed. In the safety of his car, with tears streaming down my face, I shared with him the hurt and pain my teammates had caused. He didn't say much. He didn't preach. As embarrassed as I was for crying, he didn't scold me for doing so. He didn't tell me to toughen up. He just listened. He hurt with me, and then he comforted my heart.

If encouragement is a symbolic round of applause, then comforting is a symbolic arm around the shoulder. I don't remember what my father said to me that painful afternoon, but I do remember him putting his arm around me. It was exactly what I needed. When a child is hurt, simply knowing that their dad is there and that they care is better than any words of wisdom a father can speak. The hand tool of comfort is an amazing tool that will leave a lasting impression on the heart of every child who is blessed with a father who uses it.

Precision Tools

A precision tool, such as a chisel, file, or sandpaper, can do what a power tool and hand tool cannot. They are more delicate and strategic in nature, and they are often used as finishing tools to complete a project.

The Apostle Paul uses the Greek word *marturomai*, translated here as "urging," as the final word to describe his fatherly approach to them. The word means "to exhort solemnly; to protest," and it describes an authoritative command. Today, we would express this as a *warning* or *correction*. If encouragement is a symbolic round of applause and comforting is a symbolic arm around the shoulder, then urging is a symbolic swift kick to the backside.

Urging is uniquely different from disciplining a child in response to a disobedient act. This is more than an immediate and necessary consequence – it's a deliberate confrontation about a dangerous direction. Urging is when a father sits his son down and says, "I want to talk to you about some danger signs I see concerning the attitude you're developing with your mother." It's when he takes his daughter out on a date and gently but clearly tells her, "I need to talk to you about some concerns I'm seeing with some of the choices you're making when you're around certain friends." These confrontations are like sandpaper, conversations that smooth out rough edges that are beginning to form in behavior, attitude, or habits. Sandpaper-type conversations communicate that you are genuinely concerned about what you're seeing. It also expresses that you love your child enough to smooth out this area of concern so that painful splinters do not form.

My middle daughter, Holly, is a competitive athlete with a tendency to come down extremely hard on herself when she makes a mistake while playing sports. When Holly was in eighth grade, because of her ability, she was brought up several times from her junior high basketball team to play with the high school varsity team. On one of these occasions, Holly was called up to varsity to be the back-up point guard for an important away game against their school's arch-rival. Her team was down by 17 points, but they fought back and ended up losing the game by only four points. On the bus ride home she texted me and said she'd had the "worst game ever in the history of worst games." The truth was that she entered the game late, played about three minutes, and had a turnover on a fast break. These things happen. What concerned me was her next text: "If I didn't get on the court, we had a better chance of winning."

But what bothered me even more than Holly's texts was the fact that everyone on the team, including the coaches, witnessed how hard she was on herself. On the drive home I pulled out the sandpaper. It would have been easy to write this off as an issue of simple junior high immaturity, but I knew that something deeper was going on. A pattern was beginning to form in which she lived with the daily fear of what others thought about her, putting her in bondage to their opinions. It needed correction. I began to sand, firmly and directly. I explained to my daughter that it's very difficult to enter the game cold – you haven't been in the flow and pace of the game, and mistakes often happen under these conditions. I then reminded her that she was in eighth grade, playing against seniors! I passed on her coach's praise, too – she had played well and had done what he asked her to do.

When these comments brought an "I know, but…" response, I sanded deeper. I explained that if she'd had a great game and responded with a prideful attitude, I would have been all over her case. But if she'd had an off game and responded by pouting and bellyaching about it, I'd be all over her case about that as well. I let her know that both responses were unacceptable. After communicating clearly and firmly, I set the Precision Tool down and changed the subject. If I had continued to sand by launching into a lecture or sermon, I would have caused her to tune me out, undoing the work I'd just done.

It is very tempting for parents to use Precision Tools as their instrument of choice. It is all too easy for us to teach, lecture, and preach to our kids. After all, our experience gives us the advantage when we're communicating truth to an inexperienced child or teenager. Without the balance of the Power Tool of encouragement and the Hand Tool of comfort, the Precision Tool of warning and correcting will become ineffective. Parents who do this, particularly fathers, will have kids who feel that "I can't do anything right", "They never see what I do right but always see the wrong", or "I can never please him, so why try?" This is what the Apostle Paul warns of when he cautions his readers,

> "Fathers, do not embitter your children or they will become discouraged." (Colossians 3:21)

Using the Right Tools

When it comes to tools, the first problem is not using the tools at our disposal. It doesn't matter if I have the latest and greatest tools in my garage – an unused tool is a useless tool. If I know I have a broken door and I put off fixing it, that might be considered laziness. If I have a child who needs encouragement, comfort, or correction and I refuse to do it, that might be considered neglect.

Another common mistake is choosing the wrong tool to address the problem. I've been guilty of using a tape measure to pound in a nail instead of taking the time to go to the garage and grab the hammer. As a result, I usually bend the nail and/or damage my tape measure. When we use the wrong tool with our children, the result has more lasting effects. We need to be careful not to urge when we should be encouraging, or comfort when we should be correcting. Thankfully, we have the ability to ask God for wisdom to know what to do and what to say at the appropriate moment.

There is Hope

For three years, 60-70 men would come to our church on Tuesday mornings at 5:30 a.m. for our weekly *Men's Fraternity*. This group was based around a three-year study developed by noted author Robert Lewis on how to be an authentic man, how to be successful in our relationships at home, and how to live a satisfying and full life. It was exciting to see so many, at every life stage, who were hungry to learn and grow in their roles as men. During many of our meetings, the weekly discussion topics hit the bull's eye for many men who were attempting to recover lost years or opportunities with their children.

My time leading our Men's Fraternity taught me that it is never too late for a father to have a positive impact on his children. Whether it is a father who is attempting to recover from neglecting his role as a dad to younger kids, a father who is making an effort to reestablish his relationship with his teenage children, or a father who is accepting the challenge to make up for mistakes with his grown children, there were several factors that helped these fathers succeed:

- They admitted their shortcomings as a father and asked their children for forgiveness. By humbling themselves, these fathers prepared the soil of restoration with their children.
- They understood that the effort to be a better father takes time. These fathers were aware that their initial attempts were likely to be rejected or viewed skeptically.
- They were determined not to give up. Fathers who were successful in regaining lost ground made a continual effort to encourage and engage their children.

If you are a father who desires a restored relationship with your children, regardless of their age, let me encourage you to take to heart the factors listed above, as well as allowing me to point you in the right direction: Start with the Power Tool of Encouragement. Use this tool over and over. If your child is not used to receiving encouragement from you, be patient – over time, genuine encouragement is hard to resist.

Once your child begins to warm to your words of affirmation and their skeptical heart begins to soften, you have earned the right to be heard and to use another parenting tool. Only then should you pick up the Hand Tool of Comforting. Once your efforts to comfort are received and appreciated, you have earned the right to use the Precision Tool of Urging. Resist the temptation to pull out this tool too quickly. This could cause your child to think, "Here we go again! I can't please this man," potentially unraveling all the work you have done. Tread very carefully with this tool.

Remember, restoring a relationship and earning the trust of a child takes time. By your attitude and actions you can prove to your child that you are sincere, and that you're serious about being a better father. It is never too early or too late for a father to use the right tools at the right time to strengthen his home, whether his children are very young or are now adults themselves.

If you haven't used these tools in a while, blow off the dust and begin using them today.

Small Group Questions:

1. Why do you think some fathers do not engage in the life of their family? What are the results of this lack of involvement?

2. What unique tools do fathers bring to their family? Why is it rarely too late for a father to make a significant impact on his children?

3. If encouragement is "oxygen to the soul", what are the ways in which you're using encouragement to breathe life into your children? How does encouragement from a father make an indelible imprint on life of a child?

4. How can fathers use the tool of comfort in their children's lives? Why do some fathers avoid using this tool?

5. How is correcting different from disciplining? What happens when parents use the "precision tool" of correcting as their primary parenting tool?

EPILOGUE

The Foundation

We've walked through our whole Dream House now, providing blueprints for a healthy and happy home, except for one crucial part of the home. Let me close by talking about a final aspect of every house that is rarely seen, but is nevertheless completely essential: The foundation.

The foundation determines the strength and durability of the home. If the foundation is faulty, the structure of the house will become compromised, and it will eventually be condemned. If the foundation is strong and sturdy, a house can last for many, many years and may be passed down to multiple generations.

Jesus taught a parable about the principle of firm foundations when he concluded the most famous of all sermons, the Sermon on the Mount. He said,

> *"Therefore everyone who hears these words of mine and puts them into practice is like a wise man who built his house on the rock. The rain came down, the streams rose, and the winds blew and beat against that house; yet it did not fall, because it had its foundation on the rock. But everyone who hears these words of mine and does not put them into practice is like a foolish man who built his house on sand. The rain came down, the streams rose, and the winds blew and beat against the house, and it fell with a great crash."* (Matthew 7:24-27)

A house built upon Jesus Christ is a house with a firm foundation. Every home will face storms in life, storms that can shake a family to the core. My family has faced rough times that involved death, cancer, depression, surgeries, foreclosure, and many other trials. What has kept our family together and strong

141

has been our faith in Jesus Christ. Knowing Christ, and trusting in the truth of the Bible, has supplied for us what we cannot provide for ourselves – hope, comfort, peace, and rest.

A house built on sand might appear impressive at first. It might have the latest and greatest features the best contractors can provide, but over time the sand will begin to shift and sink under the attacks of the storms of life. I have witnessed the collapse of many homes that did not have a faith to hold onto when death, disease, trials, and tribulations came their way.

The year was 1965. I was eight months old and too young to know my home was being built upon sand. My parents had been recently stunned by the breakups of several marriages within their group of close friends. My mother, who grew up with religion but without a personal relationship with God, wanted to start going back to church. My dad was more interested in playing semi-pro baseball with his buddies.

To pay the bills, my father was a milkman, rising before dawn to work the early morning shift. This was in an era when milkmen delivered fresh milk, white or chocolate, in glass containers left next to each customer's front door. One of my dad's friends, Stan Vidal, was also a milkman. These two young couples would go out to eat together or go over to each other's house from time to time to watch a ball game. One day, Stan made a statement that surprised my parents. He said with confidence that he knew for sure that he would go to heaven when he died. My parents were perplexed. "How could anyone know for sure?" they thought.

Several months later my parents and the Vidals were having dinner on a Saturday night when my mother asked her friends what they were doing the next day. They replied that they were going to church and asked my parents if they wanted to join them. My mother quickly said yes. The next day my parents found themselves pulling into a little church in San Jose called

Branham Lane Baptist Church. That morning they heard a passage explained from the book of Ephesians, which says,

> *"For it is by grace you have been saved, through faith –*
> *and this not from yourselves, it is the gift of God – not by*
> *works, so that no one can boast." (Ephesians 2:8-9)*

My mom looked closely at her Bible and thought to herself, "I've never seen this verse before. How did this get in here?" My mother left church under conviction. My dad left to play baseball.

On Wednesday night of the next week, my parents returned for a revival meeting. It was February 14, 1965. The pastor taught about sin, explaining in clear terms how everyone was a sinner. He shared from the Bible that the only cure for sin is Jesus Christ, who died on the cross to pay the penalty for our sins. Not wanting to open herself up to his relentless teasing, my mother had said nothing to my dad since the previous Sunday about what was happening in her heart. At the close of the service, the pastor invited those who wanted to accept the free gift of salvation to come down to the front. My mother immediately left her seat, coming forward in response to his invitation. When she arrived she noticed that the pastor wasn't looking at her, but seemed to be focusing behind her instead. She wondered, "Why isn't he looking at me?" He was looking at my father, who had followed my mother down the aisle.

They both met individually with church members who were waiting to talk to them, and each prayed to accept Christ as their Savior. Of all days, Valentine's Day, my father and mother gave their hearts to Jesus. Later that night my mother asked my dad what prompted him to walk forward – she was quite certain he hadn't come forward just because she did. My father responded by saying, "The man said I was a sinner. I knew I was a sinner. I had that part down." Years later, I asked my mother what, if anything, changed in their marriage following their salvation experience. She said, "Your father immediately took an interest in me." This was just the beginning.

The most significant change that Valentine night was the replacement of the sand under their marriage with the firm foundation of Jesus Christ. Upon this foundation my parents began to build their own Dream House, using the teachings of the Bible. Even with plenty of challenges and problems along the way, they built a healthy and happy home for their seven children. All seven of us are happily married and have chosen to build our homes upon the same foundation as our parents – the foundation of Jesus Christ.

What are the odds of seven children from the same family all having happy and healthy marriages these days? What are the odds that all seven of us would be building happy and healthy homes in this day and age? But it's true. Is it because we're so smart or special? Just come to one of our family reunions and you'll see right away that the answer to *that* question is a hearty "no!" Our homes are healthy and happy because of Christ. All seven of us were handed biblical blueprints from our parents, teaching us how to build a happy and healthy Dream House of our own.

You now have a set of the same blueprints I grew up with. Try them. They will work for your family. If your home is already established, take these blueprints and begin remodeling the rooms that need it most. If your family is young or just getting started, take these blueprints and build a new home. These blueprints did not originate with me. They are designed by God, who created marriage and family, and who has given us principles to make our homes healthy and happy.

May God bless you and your family as you build your own Dream House!

Small Group Questions:

1. Why is the foundation of a home so vitally important?

2. Is the foundation of your home built on sand, or on the solid rock of Jesus Christ?

3. If your foundation is built on sand, will you pray right now to receive Christ as your Savior? Ask Him to forgive you of your sins and trust in Jesus Christ, by faith, to be your Savior.

ABOUT THE AUTHOR

Since 2005, Barry has served as the senior pastor of GracePoint Church in Bremerton, WA. He grew up in a large, loud, and loving family along with six other siblings. He and his wife Candy have been happily married for 25 years, and they have three children. His family loves to laugh, watch football, devour barbecue, and be in the sun as much as possible.

Barry was a youth pastor for 20 years before becoming the senior pastor at GracePoint. He served in two churches in Washington and concluded his student ministry days as the high school pastor at First Evangelical Free Church in Fullerton, California. He received his formal education at Liberty University and Talbot Seminary.

Contact Barry
Barry has a great blog that you can find at www.barrybandara.com. You can also follow him on Twitter @barry49er. If you wish to contact Barry or inquire about his availability as a speaker, you can email him at barry@gracepointkitsap.com.

Who or what is Overboard Books?

Overboard Books publishes quality books that are designed to assist in getting Christians overboard — out of the boat. It's the publishing arm of Overboard Ministries, whose mission is based on Matthew 14. In that chapter we find the familiar story of Jesus walking on water while His disciples were in a boat. It was the middle of the night, the water was choppy and Jesus freaked out His followers who thought He was a ghost. When they realized it was Him, Peter asked to come out to Him on the water, and he actually walked on top of the water like Jesus.

But what truly captivates me is thought of the other eleven disciples who remained in the boat. I've often wondered how many of them questioned that move in the years to come? How many of them wished they hadn't stayed in the boat but had instead gone overboard with Peter? Overboard Ministries aims to help Christians get out of boat and live life for Christ out on the water where He is. We hope and pray that each book published by Overboard Ministries will stir believers to jump overboard and live life all-out for God, full of joy and free from the regret of "I wish I had…"

What we do
Overboard Books is the publishing arm of Overboard Ministries. Overboard Ministries emerged in the summer of 2010 as an umbrella ministry for several concepts my wife and I were developing. One of those concepts was a book ministry that would help other Christian authors get published. I experienced a lot of frustration while passing my first manuscript around. I kept getting rejection letters that were kindly written, but each echoed the same sentiment: "We love this book. If you were already a published author, we would love to publish it." They were nice letters, but that didn't make the rejection any easier or the logic less frustrating.

Out of that came the audacious idea to start our own "publishing company." I put that in quotes because I want people to know a couple of things. First of all, we're not a traditional publishing company like most people envision when they hear the name. We don't have a printing press in our garage, and we don't have a marketing team. Basically, we're a middle-man who absorbs most of the cost of publishing in order to help you get published, while making sure the majority of profits end up in your pocket, not ours.

Our desire is to keep costs to a bare minimum for each author. (As of this writing, there is only a minimal contract fee when your manuscript is accepted.) We provide resources and ideas to help authors work on marketing, while also providing the editor and graphic design artist at our expense. We subcontract out the printing, which speeds up the time it takes to move from final draft to bound book. Since we don't have much overhead we can keep our expenses low, allowing seasoned authors, or first-time authors like me, the opportunity to profit from their writing. This makes it possible for authors to publish more books while continuing in their current jobs or ministries.

Contact us

If you are interested in other books or learning about other authors from Overboard Books, please visit our website at www.overboardministries.com and click on the "Overboard Books" link. If you are an author interested in publishing with us, please visit our site and check out the "Authors" tab. There you will find a wealth of information that will help you understand the publishing process and how we might be a good fit for you. If we're not a fit for you, we'll gladly share anything we've learned that might be helpful to you as you pursue publishing through other means.

Thank you

Thanks for supporting our work and ministry. If you believe this book was helpful to you, tell someone about it! Or better yet, buy them a copy of their own! We completely depend on word-of-mouth grassroots marketing to help spread the word about Overboard Ministries and its publications. Please share our website with others and encourage them to purchase the materials that will help them live "overboard" lives for Christ.

May God bless you as you grab the side of boat, take a deep breath…and jump onto the sea!

Suggested Resources

Here is a list of suggested resources that Candy and I have found helpful in our parenting. Although this list is not exhaustive, we hope these resources will give you tools to better parent your children.

Apologetics
- *Don't Check Your Brains at the Door* – Josh McDowell
- *More Than a Carpenter* – Josh McDowell
- *The Case for Christ* (Student Edition) – Lee Strobel
- *The Case for a Creator* (Student Edition) – Lee Strobel
- *The Case for Faith* (Student Edition) – Lee Strobel

Discipleship
- *Keys for Kids* – CBH Ministries
- *The Search for Significance* (Student Edition) – Robert S. McGee
- *God, What's Your Name?* – Kay Arthur & Janna Arndt
- *Stepping Up: A Journey Through the Psalms of Ascent* – Beth Moore

Purity
- *Passport2Purity* – Dennis & Barbara Rainey
- *Authentic Beauty* – Leslie Ludy
- *Lady in Waiting* – Debby Jones & Jackie Kendall
- *Every Young Man's Battle* – Stephen Arterburn, Fred Stoeker, & Mike Yorkey

For Mothers
- *5 Conversations You Must Have with Your Daughter* – Vicki Courtney
- *Your Girl* – Vicki Courtney
- *Girl Talk: Mother Daughter Conversations on Biblical Womanhood* – Carolyn Mahaney & Nicole Mahaney Whitacre
- *Here for You: Creating a Mother-Daughter bond that lasts a lifetime* – Susie Shellenberger & Kathy Gowler

For Fathers
- *Raising a Modern Day Knight* – Dr. Robert Lewis
- *Questions for My Father* – Vincent Staniforth
- *Interviewing Your Daughter's Date* – Dennis Rainey
- *Tender Warrior* – Stu Weber

General
- *The Blessing* – John Trent & Gary Smalley
- *Shepherding a Child's Heart* – Tedd Tripp
- *Heaven for Kids* – Randy Alcorn
- *Laugh Your Way to a Better Marriage (DVD)* – Mark Gungor – www.laughyourway.com
- *Weekend to Remember* (Marriage Weekend Retreat) – www.familylife.com
- *Character First* – 36 Character Traits studies – http://store.characterfirst.com/collections/elementary/products/teachers-guide-kit-elem

End Notes

[1] United States. Supreme Court of the United States of America. "Stone v Graham, 449 U.S. 39" 17 Nov. 1980. 15 Aug, 2011 http://supreme.justia.com/us/449/39/case.html.

[2] *What a Girl Wants*. Dir. Dennie Gordon. Perf. Amand Bynes, Colin Firth, Kelly Preston. Warner Bros. Pictures, (2003). DVD.

[3] *Ethics USA*. September, 1999. National Character Education Center. 12, July 2011. http://www.ethicsusa.com/article.cfm?ID=76.

[4] *Laugh Your Way to a Better Marriage*. Mark Gungor. Laugh Your Way, (2010). DVD.

[5] Mandell, Johnathan. "Mom's work would bring in $138.095 a year" *CNN.com. CNN*, 3 May, 2007. Web. August, 2011.

[6] Stanley, Andy. *The Principle of the Path*. Nashville, Thomas Nelson. 2008.

[7] Weber, Stu. *Tender Warrior* (135-136). Sisters, Multnomah Publishers, 1996. Used by permission.

CPSIA information can be obtained
at www.ICGtesting.com
Printed in the USA
FSHW010956160620
71243FS

9 780983 456810